Here on Lake Hallie

Here on Lake Hallie

In Praise of Barflies, Fix-It Guys, and Other Folks in Our Hometown

Patti See

WISCONSIN HISTORICAL SOCIETY PRESS

Published by the Wisconsin Historical Society Press
Publishers since 1855

The Wisconsin Historical Society helps people connect to the past by collecting, preserving, and sharing stories. Founded in 1846, the Society is one of the nation's finest historical institutions.
Join the Wisconsin Historical Society: wisconsinhistory.org/membership

Printed in Wisconsin, USA
Cover design and typesetting by Sara DeHaan

26 25 24 23 22   1 2 3 4 5

Library of Congress Cataloging-in-Publication Data

Names: See, Patti, author.
Title: Here on Lake Hallie : in praise of barflies, fix-it guys, and other folks in our
    hometown / Patti See.
Other titles: In praise of barflies, fix-it guys, and other folks in our hometown
Description: [Madison] : Wisconsin Historical Society Press, [2022]
Identifiers: LCCN 2021043875 (print) | LCCN 2021043876 (e-book) |
    ISBN 9780870209918 (paperback) | ISBN 9780870209925 (epub)
Subjects: LCSH: See, Patti—Family—Anecdotes. | See, Patti—Friends and
    associates—Anecdotes. | Chippewa River Valley (Wis.)—Social life and cus-
    toms—20th century—Anecdotes. | Chippewa River Valley (Wis.)—Social life
    and customs—21st century—Anecdotes. | Chippewa River Valley (Wis.)—
    History, Local. | Chippewa River Valley (Wis.)—Biography—Anecdotes.
Classification: LCC F587.C5 S44 2022 (print) | LCC F587.C5 (e-book) | DDC
    977.5/44—dc23/eng/20211109
LC record available at https://lccn.loc.gov/2021043875
LC e-book record available at https://lccn.loc.gov/2021043876

For Alex and for Noah, Dan, & Laura

Credits

"If She Dies, She Dies" (as "She Dies, She Dies") originally appeared in *5ive for Women* magazine.

"On Thin Ice" (as "Fire on Ice" and "The News from Lake Hallie"), "Never Afraid" (as "Lessons Learned from Best Friends" and "Recalling Friendship and Summer Nights on Lake Hallie"), "Man with Dog," "Fine Music," "Secret Spaces," "The Birdman of Chippewa Falls" (as "The 100 Year-Old Bird Man of Chippewa Falls"), and "Family Delicacy" (as "Squirrel Eating") originally appeared on *Wisconsin Life*.

"Cautionary Tales" (as "Ice Fishing on Lake Hallie"), "Living on Summer Time," "Egg Laying," "Forward" (as "Forward Has Many Meanings"), "Why I Revere My Septic Guy," "The Eagle Man of Eau Claire," "Date Cutters" (as "Portrait of a Date Cutter"), "The Bird Man of Chippewa Falls," "Our Miss Victory," "Lake Hallie Spirits," "Fish Fry at Irvine," "No Green Bananas," "Everything Must Go," "Cribbage Family" (as "Cribbage a Family Affair"), "Goodbye 617," "Firebugs" (as "Call of the Firebugs"), "The Cruelest Month" (as "February: The Cruelest Month"), "Our Old Town" (as "Our Old Town Chippewa Falls"), "Shake-a-Day," "Get Your Blue Mind On," "The Heart Has Many Doors" (as "Good Riddance 2020"), and "Witness to History" originally appeared in the Eau Claire *Leader-Telegram* and in *Country Today*.

"Joyful Mysteries" (as "Joyful Mystery") originally appeared in *Take Care: Tales, Tips, and Love from Women Caregivers*, edited by Elayne Clift.

"Tonight at Dad's," "Tavern Tour," and "Patti Barge" (as "Everything Happened or Nothing Did") originally appeared in *Volume One Magazine*.

"Mourning Portrait" originally appeared in *What Remains: The Many Ways We Say Goodbye, An Anthology*, edited by Sandi Gelles-Coles and Kenneth Salzmann.

"Washtub" originally appeared in *Months to Years* literary journal.

Note: Some of these essays were cut, edited, and/or combined for this book.

Contents

Let's Stop Time

Wedding photo of Patti See and Bruce Taylor at their house on Lake Hallie.
PHOTO BY CELIA JOACHIM

If She Dies, She Dies

In June, my car was broadsided on the highway near my home. The impact crushed my driver's side and pummeled my head off the window. As I waited for an ambulance, a pair of friendly power walkers asked to pray over me and offered to call my husband. I couldn't speak to tell them "no husband." At the hospital, the chaplain said she and my "husband" Bruce were praying for me.

Months earlier, when Bruce had first talked of marriage, I teased, "A tattoo will last longer." I soon found myself with his signature across my hip. Our tattoo artist told us that getting a partner's name on your body ruins most relationships. "Winona Forever," Bruce and I said—at the same time. It was nearly magical.

A day after my accident, my neck and shoulder aching, I sat in our yard in a lawn chair while Bruce made dinner inside. This day, like all of my others, a gift. All I could think was how much I wanted to be here with this man I adore. I went into the bathroom and wrote "PLEASE MARRY ME" in black permanent marker across my lower back and midsection. I knew if I didn't do it immediately, I'd chicken out. Not that I'm afraid of commitment, or even of being with my true love, but it is difficult to take that leap of faith after a divorce.

When I was twenty-two, the question was popped for me by a surprise pregnancy. I had no fantasy of how a man would ask me to marry him; I only knew this scenario was not remotely close to what I thought it might be. We were good Catholic kids—of course we got married. I was carrying the child of the man I loved. Still, when I look back at the girl I was then, with more than two decades of hindsight, one word comes to mind: doomed.

Years later, going through a divorce was like jumping off a sinking ship, only everyone you know wonders what you did to damage the hull or to deserve a life raft. The worst day of my life was telling my nine-year-old son that his dad and I were separating. As Raymond Carver wrote about his own dismantling marriage, "I'd rather take poison than go through that again."

A whole day passed before Bruce noticed the proposal inked on my body. He lifted my shirt and read slowly, "SE MAR? What's that?"

I hadn't considered the size of my handwritten letters on my torso. I'd just picked up a marker and started writing—in reverse in the bathroom mirror. The *SE* of *PLEASE* and *MAR* of *MARRY* blended together around the edge of my stomach.

I pointed out each word individually. "Oh," Bruce said. "I thought those were marks leftover from when you got x-rayed in the emergency room."

We laughed and laughed.

"This is a proposal," I said finally.

"Yes," he said solidly. Surely.

I'm forty-three and Bruce is sixty-four, so becoming a bride likely means I will become a widow. A joyful marriage awaits, but perhaps so does eventual tragedy. Bruce tells me that worn-out joke about a ninety-year-old guy who marries a much younger woman. His doctor says, "Somebody could get hurt," and the old guy responds: "If she dies, she dies."

We decide to be secretly engaged and elope to Las Vegas in January—six months away—then throw a big party in the spring when all of our four kids can be there.

Suddenly it's November, and I realize I have to be prepared for a wedding in less than eight weeks. I start shopping for a dress.

A family picture from my wedding some twenty years ago hangs in our hallway: me in my mother's wedding dress, surrounded by my parents and siblings. One day, many months engaged, I realize that the reason I haven't found the perfect dress for my upcoming wedding is that I wore it for my first. What would Emily Post say? Is it beyond tacky to wear the same dress twice?

I email my friend Barbara, whose study of women's material culture means she can give me better advice than anyone. "That dress is about you and your mom," she writes, "not about any groom."

I decide to remake the dress: shorten it and take off the lace, perhaps change the neckline. I contact a woman who worked on the wedding dress of a friend of a friend. Standing in this stranger's hallway, large mirrors on both sides of me, I think what a kick my mom would get out of me in her sixty-four-year-old dress and my new red velvet boots. I tell Sue, the seamstress, that I believe the dress is handmade, but my mom is in late-stage Alzheimer's, and I don't have anyone to ask.

Sue says, "I wore my mom's dress, too."

I tear up. For maybe the first time since my mom forgot who I am, years ago now, I miss her. I cry all the way home. I realize it's time to tell our family and friends about our engagement.

I text my best friend, Karen, and she immediately texts back, "First smile today thinking of you in that dress and red boots and thinking what your mom would say."

～

After our ceremony at a Las Vegas chapel, I order us drinks at the hotel bar while Bruce uses the restroom. A guy two stools away eyes my wedding dress. "Got married, huh?" he says.

I nod. I tell him about being stranded at our chapel in a questionable neighborhood and waiting for a cab that never came, about catching a ride with a couple who remarried each other after being divorced for two decades.

The guy at the bar is fifty or so, with a graying goatee and a construction worker's well-muscled arms. He says, "I thought about doing it again, but who would want an old guy like me?"

Bruce comes back from the bathroom and sits beside me. The guy looks at us and says to me, "Well, apparently you." He laughs nervously.

Bruce's face questions: *What did I miss?*

I say, "He's wondering who would marry an old guy."

Bruce says to everyone at the bar, "She knows I'll die before we get sick of each other."

We all raise our drinks in a toast, and our new friend laughs as if he's never heard anything so funny or so true.

On Thin Ice

Our neighbor Helen Sabaska says that Bruce and I live "across the street." The lake is narrow enough for us to yell from our house to hers. When the water freezes, we *are* across the street, and the lake becomes a village of shacks with an ice road down the middle—many feet of snow rutted and trampled by vehicles filled with fishermen out here to catch northern or bass, though most settle for panfish.

Each winter, our neighbor Larry Luedtke measures the ice so we know when to walk across Lake Hallie from our dock to his. A few years ago, I saw him out on the perfectly clear ice; no snow had fallen during the consecutive nights of deep freeze that solidified maybe two inches. I stood on my dock, too afraid to go out where he'd drilled a hole and dropped a line. He generally comes over to tell me the ice is safe; then I walk in exactly his boot prints on my first few times out alone.

"Let me take your picture," I yelled to him. I wasn't sure he could see his reflection on the mirror-like ice.

Just as I was about to snap the photo, he pulled a three-foot northern pike up through that tiny hole. I swear the fins touched both sides. I jostled my phone. I've seen fish caught on ice but nothing so big and startling as this. Once his mammoth was off the hook, I snapped a photo of Larry proudly holding it. No matter how much I wanted to see that fish, I still would not leave my dock.

Larry's next-door neighbors Dave and Marion Mecikalski bought their house in 1967. That winter on Lake Hallie, Dave pushed his flat-bottomed boat onto the ice, drilled a hole, and fished over the bow. Our first winter here, in 2010, Helen told me about Dave "ice fishing" from his johnboat, wearing a life preserver over his parka. She said, "It was the funniest thing I have ever seen."

This year, Dave tells me the same story and adds a part I'd never heard. Another neighbor, now long dead, came out to see what Dave was up to, and the guy fell through ice. The moral: don't laugh at newcomers, and respect the springs that feed this lake.

~

That first winter, the first time I walked on the ice to visit my neighbors was on Christmas Eve.

Karen Sabaska, my best friend since childhood, arrived at her parents' for early holiday cheer. Her sons set up a hockey game and took turns shooting into the portable nets. I went out on my deck to watch. The swish of their skates on the fresh ice reminded me of being a kid here with Karen.

Later, she met me in the middle of the lake to walk with me back to her parents' house. I stopped moving when I heard what sounded like a gun shot. "Listen," I said. The way we both froze, we could have been caught in a game of "statue tag."

Karen screamed, "Keep going! The ice is cracking."

We ran to safety, near the hockey nets close to shore. We giggled and giggled.

"Your face!" She laughed some more, doubled over with mittens on her knees.

Larry tells us that a cracking sound doesn't mean the ice is splitting beneath us; most likely, the sound is just traveling underneath the ice as it shifts and contracts, like plate tectonics.

After a while, Karen offered to walk me back to my house. "If you go in, I go in," she said.

"Okay," I said, "but you walk ahead of me"—something I might have said to her forty years earlier when she ice skated and I ran along beside her in my rainbow-patterned moon boots.

As a kid, I often ice fished with my parents. I sat patiently on an overturned bucket and stared through a hole no bigger than a Frisbee. But the highlight for me was always a roaring fire on the ice, not lacing a waxy—an enormous maggot—onto a hook with my cold fingers or attempting to cut through a foot of ice with a hand auger. Back then, I also enjoyed roasting wieners in the black smoke of a fire fueled by Styrofoam plates and skitching down a snowy street holding onto a car bumper—risks I'd never take as an adult.

That first winter we lived on Lake Hallie, just five miles south of where I grew up in Chippewa Falls, Wisconsin, I researched how burning logs create enough ash to form a layer between the hot coals and the ice. To appease my husband, I agreed to build our fire close enough to shore that if the ice cracked and we all tumbled through (Bruce's fear), we'd just stand up to save ourselves.

In January, on the day of our first fire-on-ice gathering, my nineteen-year-old son and I constructed the fire together long before guests arrived. Alex would leave for basic training in a few weeks, and that night was his send-off, so his aunts and uncles and cousins and grandpa could all have a chance to say goodbye.

Alex and I carried down brittle pine branches and chunks of

oak from our covered woodpile. He carefully made a log-cabin structure and narrated as he added log after log: "You want good air movement, and you don't want the whole thing to collapse." I'd never thought of either of those points. That's why he's the Eagle Scout and ROTC cadet, while I'm the writer who pontificates about the grandeur of bonfires on ice from her youth.

That night, I had a few surprises for Alex: a cake adorned with plastic army men and a shoveled path across the lake lined with dozens of luminaria to light our neighbors' way. This is a fancy name for paper lunch sacks full of sand with candle stubs inside. But when the luminaria were lit on that dark January night, they lived up to their name.

My son was a man, no longer wowed by things that might impress a boy. Still, I wanted his party to be memorable—whether that meant Alex laughing as his tipsy grandpa licked frosting off of plastic GI Joe boots or Alex recalling a glowing bonfire on ice weeks later when he'd be sweltering in Fort Benning, Georgia, for four months.

Our fire took a little nudging to light, but when it finally caught, all guests *ooh*ed and *ahh*ed. They stamped their feet and drank their Leinenkugel's and passed around peppermint schnapps with hot chocolate.

Kids snapped pictures and instantly posted them online. "It's a fire . . . on a lake!" one wrote. This made me smile. What was a common occurrence in my childhood—a break from the monotony of ice fishing—was now a novelty worthy of tweeting.

～

That March, our insurance agent called to see if he could park in our driveway for the annual ice fishing contest. When he arrived early on Saturday morning, Bruce warned him about the pockets of open water along the shore.

This guy's livelihood was risk management. Who better to

decide when to avoid thin ice? Bruce stood at the window and watched Mr. Agent step off the dock and take tentative steps.

"He went in!" Bruce shouted to me. "He's up to his waist."

Before our agent pulled himself out of the lake, my phone rang. "Your friend fell in," Larry said. "No one should be out on the ice today."

"Yep," I said. "We told him."

Bruce invited Mr. Agent inside to change clothes or simply warm up. "No thanks," he said. "I'm gonna try a spot closer to the bar." He headed to his truck with his five-gallon bucket full of gear.

When I witness newsworthy events out here on frozen Lake Hallie, I always call Larry or Dave. They see exactly what I do but from a slightly different angle: otters playing in open water, an eagle lurking over an ice fisherman's abandoned hole, a tricked-out ice fishing shack with one too many tip-ups.

When one or the other answers the phone, I no longer feel compelled to say, "It's Patti from across the lake." I simply launch into: "Are you looking out your window? You should be!"

One time, we watched a leather-clad dude pop wheelies on his motorbike up and down the perfectly smooth ice. Another time, we stared at a muskrat diving into the frigid water, bringing up weed after weed, and eating them on the edge of the ice. We'd leave our lookouts to take a nap or have lunch or get the mail, but when we returned to our windows, that muskrat would still be there—nibbling on weeds and throwing its leftovers into a slimy pile.

Once, I saw a guy in a bright red jacket pedaling a black mountain bike in knee-high rubber boots. I could only watch, dumbfounded, as he pulled a child splayed out on his belly on a saucer sled. This was mid-December, and we'd recently had rain. I would not have set foot on the lake, much less ridden a bike. And certainly not a bike pulling a kid. I could have called social services, but we all have our memorable stories about being on thin ice.

I snapped as many photos as I could while these strangers glided by. I couldn't see the kid's face—with his hood up and belly down, flying over a thin sheet of ice clearer than an ice cube—but he had to be grinning.

Cautionary Tales

My husband and I watch the daily movement on freezing-thawing-refreezing Lake Hallie. First come what Bruce calls "Jesus geese," who appear to waddle on water those mornings when the rime is just thick enough for migrating birds to land on the lake. Then come the risk-takers. Last November, I could launch a kayak off our dock into chilly water and watch teens ice fishing on the frozen middle of the lake.

Now we see the diehards of mid-March, a different breed of adventurer willing to slosh through five inches of wet slurry to get to a prime fishing spot.

I've come to recognize Lake Hallie's winter sounds: the groan and boom of shifting ice, the motorized whine of a power auger. Most weekends, I awaken to fishermen checking their tip-ups right outside my bedroom window.

One recent morning, I noticed a lone figure in the distance, a Yeti lookalike pulling a sled of fishing gear. From my toasty kitchen, I could see the thermometer read fourteen below zero. Is this obsession with ice fishing like deer fever, that tunnel vision that affects hunters? I remember what my friend Bill Nolte once said about smokers outside his bar, the Joynt, on a frigid Saturday night: "I wish I loved anything that much."

I grew up hearing our across-the-lake neighbor's cautionary tales. Helen Sabaska's ten-year-old nephew, Carter, once fell through thin ice, and another kid plucked him out. Fifty-two years later, Carter tells me that going home wearing his seven-year-old girl cousin's sweatpants was more traumatic than busting through the ice.

In mid-December of 1993, Helen's son Tom heard cries for help from an eighty-year-old fisherman. The *Chippewa Herald* reported that a hole in the ice kept getting larger as Clyde Stetzer floundered and looked for something to cling to. About the cracked ice, Clyde said, "I'd walked that way once, but it just opened up and let me in." Tom grabbed a canoe, slid it out twenty feet from shore, and somehow managed to rescue this stranger. Once Clyde was inside Helen's warm house, he told a reporter, "I'm a lucky boy to be here today. The water was pretty cold."

These early-season mishaps explain why local taverns wait until the first and third Saturdays in February for their ice fishing contests. Lake Hallie Sportsman's Club has sponsored one since 1980, and Slim's Lake Hallie Tavern has had one since 2008. Both offer prizes for the fattest bluegill, crappie, perch, northern, and bass, then hold post-fishing raffles back at the bar.

People set up camp for a day: lawn chairs, coolers, and five-gallon buckets of beer and gear. A folding table goes up for registration and fish weigh-in, a Porta-Potty is unloaded, and a chili dog/beverage cart tools around. This year, the ice isn't thick enough for vehicles heavier than snowmobiles, three-wheelers, or gators, which resemble a swarm of mini army jeeps.

One woman tells me her kids are inside their pop-up tent viewing a small screen of crappie and perch swimming beneath the ice. I marvel at her tiny fish finder camera snaked down a hole at my feet. This technology is supposed to be used for catching fish, not just watching them. It's a little like playing a videogame when the real thing is just steps away.

A group of three generations reels in a seven-plus-pound northern on Grandma's pole. She tells me her arms got tired, so her son hauled it out. Her little granddaughter says, confidently, "We're the winner."

The week between contests, a minivan breaks through the lake just down from our house. The thirty-something driver heard cracking ice in the wee-hour darkness and instinctively opened his car door. He reached toward the back seat but could not grab his dog before his vehicle sank. He struggled out of the icy water and walked nearly a mile down the frozen lake to the Sportsman's Club. When he knocked on a window for help, his hair was covered in icicles.

The next night, a tow-truck driver stops at our house to ask if he can use our land for vehicle recovery come daylight. He also wants to know the exact location of the springs that feed Lake Hallie along our shore. I point toward Helen's house: "Right across from that one."

Two days later, a salvage crew launches from Helen's level land rather than our steep embankment and avoids our shoreline's weaker ice by dragging the vehicle, while it's still underwater, to the middle of the lake for extraction. I can't wait to witness this, but I have to work. Karen reports to her mom's, then sends hourly texts and photos my way.

Neighbors gather as three guys in yellow vests chainsaw through inches of ice that have formed over the sunken vehicle. The diver looks like he's swimming in a glass of large ice cubes. He slips underwater to fasten a winch hook to the minivan's front seatbelts. Old-timers say this is the sixth vehicle to break through since 1967, another reason those who've lived here the longest will never drive on Lake Hallie.

A johnboat in February can only mean a rescue or a death. Eventually, the diver surfaces with the owner's dog. Karen's photo shows the pet wrapped in a tarp and left on the ice. At the end of the day, crew members will load the bundle onto the wrecker last.

My retired firefighter brother, Joe, comes to our place three different times to watch and wait, then returns home when nothing much happens. In a weird telephone game that could only occur in this century, Karen sends photo updates to me in Eau Claire, I forward them to Joe in Chippewa Falls, and then he shows up to visit Bruce, who's been periodically watching the action through binoculars from our Lake Hallie kitchen. After work, I rush outside to witness the final retrieval.

Ten hours after the men positioned a six-foot beam through the minivan's busted-out back windows—from a distance, this looks like a Matchbox car skewered with a popsicle stick—the Honda Odyssey is towed on its top across the ice to a wrecker idling on Helen's shore. Given the daylong spectacle, Bruce jokes it's like we're watching the raising of the *Titanic*. More likely, it would be the *Loraine*—a wrecked early-twentieth-century steamboat—or even a bootlegger's still, thrown into the lake when Prohibition feds got too close. Both are hidden beneath the ice. Since the winter of 1843, when Blue Mills loggers took their first cautious steps onto the spring-fed holding pond that would later be named Lake Hallie, 178 years of risk-takers have shared the same sentiment: if not "Oh, what the hell," then a more courageous, "Why not?"

Groundhog Wars

One March morning years ago, I was scolding my husband for some small thing he did or did not do. I grabbed my car keys for a dramatic exit and noticed two woodchucks in our yard. The smaller one charged toward the bigger one, who did a sidestep dance to retreat.

"Come look at this," I called to Bruce. Big took a few steps in the direction of Small, who advanced again. Bruce and I stood watching what was likely more of a mating dance than a smackdown. I put my arm around him. Bruce said, "They fight just like us." We both crumpled into laughter.

That was our honeymoon phase with our male and female woodchucks, both of whom we call Chuckie. A woodchuck doesn't actually chuck wood, so there's no need to ponder how much it would. Woodchucks do, however, gnaw on our cedar steps, eat our flowers, dig a labyrinth of tunnels under our garage, and produce up to six kits a season. The two of us and our woodchucks are definitely past the seven-year itch.

Until we moved to rural Lake Hallie in 2010, I had no idea that a woodchuck is a groundhog is a whistle pig.

Sun Prairie citizens can thank Eau Claire artist Ira Bennett for proclaiming their town state headquarters for Groundhog Day when he created holiday postcards to commemorate various cities for Wisconsin's centennial in 1948. You can see why he

chose Port Washington for President's Day and Independence
for the Fourth of July. But the Sun Prairie connection is a bit of a
stretch: Ira and his young son reasoned that on Groundhog Day,
the whistle pig either does or does not see his shadow when the
sun comes up on the prairie, so this town, located thirty minutes
north of Madison, was chosen. A group of locals soon christened
Sun Prairie the Groundhog Capital of the World, much to the
disdain of one Pennsylvania city that thought it had a monopoly
on this marmot holiday.

Though Punxsutawney Phil may be more famous—and 134
years old—his predictions for the end of winter are only 39 percent accurate compared with Sun Prairie Jimmy's prognostica-
tions, correct 80 percent of the time. Here lies just one cause of
the ongoing groundhog war between these two cities.

This year in the Chippewa Valley, cold and snow have re-
mained for well over four weeks since February 2. But I'm not
blaming a rodent.

Every winter, mice and chipmunks sneak into my warm basement or garage. We kill them in traps and throw them outside for
the foxes. Those critters do minimal damage, like building nests
on the engine of our SUV, but a troop of groundhogs—however
cute—can cause major harm to structures.

Last spring, we hired Advanced Concrete and Repairs to drill
holes in our uneven garage floor and inject cement under the concrete slab. You may have heard the company's radio commercial
for mud-jacking: "We're here to pump it up!"—a riff on "Pumping
Up with Hans & Franz" from 1980s *Saturday Night Live.*

Cement guru Franz (his real name) voices his own commer-
cials, so when we talked in person, all I could hear was that *SNL*
weightlifting Franz. "Something tunneled under your garage,"
he told me.

"Woodchucks," I said.

"You *knew* you had something living there?" he asked. I can imagine how Franz might deal with animals messing with his concrete in rural Mondovi. The other Franz's fake German accent rattles in my head: "Hear me now and believe me later."

According to the Wisconsin Department of Natural Resources, it's legal to hunt "nuisance animals" year-round on your property; they can be euthanized or relocated. Because woodchuck dens can undermine and weaken foundations, driveways, and rock walls, permission from a property owner must be granted before any animal can be released. In other words, who wants your whistle pig?

We lived in harmony with generations of Chuckies before realizing the potential destruction they could cause, like displacing up to seven hundred pounds of dirt to create a series of connected underground chambers for food storage, waste, and nesting.

Once Franz's crew started to mud-jack, they actually ran out of cement mix. The woodchuck burrow was *that* big. "We never know what we'll find," he said.

After the under-garage rodent mansion had been sealed in, I soon saw Chuckie sunning himself on the patio just feet from my back door: flat on his stomach, limbs splayed out like a spring breaker working on his tan. When I opened the screen, he turned one eye in my direction, as if to say, "You again." He didn't budge until I approached, then he scurried behind the stairs. The next day, I found a heap of dirt and sand near the steps.

By midsummer, I caught him nibbling my lace bush near our foundation, then retreating beneath the stairs attached to our house. Something had to be done.

Around this time, Bruce's daughter, Laura, and her husband, Ben, bought their first home. Surprise: woodchucks lived beneath their shed. Ben set a trap with kale—they live in Madison, after all—and somehow two woodchucks ended up in one cage. Each time Ben went near it, the two Chuckies brawled with each other. In a weird design flaw, the trap had no handle. How could they carry it without getting bitten? When Critter Ridder didn't answer their after-hours message, Laura found a local guy. He picked up their cage bare-handed and threw it in the back of his pickup. I thought the young couple was being city soft, until I caught my own teeth-baring, wolverine-clawed woodchuck two months later.

While Bruce was out running errands, I set our live trap and made a trail of irresistible cantaloupe hunks leading into the back of the trap.

Chuckie poked his head out from the steps.

I continued my Sunday chores. Carrying laundry past the window, I saw him scooping up fruit. When he nabbed the last piece, the gate slammed shut behind him. Chuckie turned and head-butted the door. Even through my closed windows, I could hear his snarling.

I thought of all the times when I'd had big ideas, but when the time came for action, my heart had galloped in my chest to the beat of one final syllable: "No."

I grabbed the only twin bed sheet I could find, one with smiley faces on it—a detail that still makes me cringe—and I crept out the side door and threw it over the cage. Chuckie calmed down.

I waited for Bruce and his sons. None of them are take-charge guys who would "Little Lady" me out of the way, which was, honestly, exactly what I wanted.

Soon, I sat at the kitchen counter across from my three Taylor guys. Each of us uttered a plan that reflected our personalities.

Laid-back Bruce: "Let's just leave Chuckie there; he's not going anywhere."

Soft-hearted Dan: "Can't we call someone?"

Logical Noah: "Google says bubble gum will kill a woodchuck."

Git-'er-done Patti: "Let's finish this beer and deal with it then."

Never Afraid

I sat behind Karen in Miss Rhinehart's second grade class: Sabaska, See. She asked if she could borrow a comb; I told her I'd never used one. She looked at my frizzy hair and laughed. That was over forty years ago, and we're still best friends. We've known each other through bad plaid and stone-washed denim, unfortunate haircuts and worse prom dresses. We have spent enough time with each other's parents and children that we worry about them as if they were our own.

The summer I turned seven, Karen and I were swimming in front of her house, and I went under. She pulled me out of a sandy drop-off by my hair. The next year, when *Jaws* caused a "don't go in the water" craze, she scared me with just a few beats of the theme song. *Da-dum. Da-dum.* I'm convinced she saved me from drowning just to terrorize me with shark threats a year later. Of course, all I might have felt brush against my legs in Lake Hallie was an overgrown carp or a colorful box turtle.

Chippewa Falls recently had the coldest winter on record since 1978. That year, extreme temperatures and a heating-oil shortage meant that at Holy Ghost Grade School the thermostat was set so low kids wore mittens or gloves in class. I still remember trying to hold a pencil in my homemade mitts and do timed multiplication tests—a little like changing a pillowcase while wearing boxing gloves.

Forty-plus years later, the Wisconsin winters still wear us down, so much so that I use a vacation day in late April to stay home because the ice on Lake Hallie has finally thawed. On this Friday morning, I paddle around the entire lake for the first time of the season. As I come around the bend, I spot Karen's car in her parents' driveway. I call her cell phone. "Come out and talk to me," I say.

I sit in my kayak in the ankle-deep water, and she stands on the bank a few feet from me. Not for the first time, she teases me about wearing a lifejacket on one of the shallowest lakes in Wisconsin. She looks beyond my kayak. "What's that?" she says. "Behind you." I shrug. I'm guessing it's another turtle, but I don't say anything.

"I wouldn't worry," she says. "I don't *think* it can chew through a plastic kayak." Same intonation and expression as when we were kids.

Once, when we were chased up a tree by a neighborhood Doberman, she made this same face right before we both ran. The *Jaws* theme extended to dogs as well. *Da-dum. Da-dum.*

"You've been doing this to me since we were seven. Stop it," I say.

She giggles. "What?"

"You're not going to scare me anymore."

Karen lets out the biggest howl of laughter I've heard in a long time. She tries to say something but can't form words. "Well," she says finally, "just look how strong it made you."

⌇

I lived in town near school, and Karen was a bus kid. When we were twelve, she often came home with me from evening basketball practice. On those short walks, I scared her with tales of our eccentric neighbor, Hank "Oink" Purvis. He was a shell-shocked

World War II veteran, more like Boo Radley than Ed Gein, but she sprinted past his ramshackle house anyway. This nearly made up for every walk we took in the woods at her place when she would pause to say, "What was that?" before dashing away, leaving me in the darkness.

Teasing was love for us. When we were a little older, Karen dumped me out of the canoe each time we went for a ride, often in front of the cabin where I now live.

Back then, how could I have imagined staying here? I had the world ahead of me and, like most teenagers I knew, I believed the first step would be away from the Chippewa Valley. After I moved to Lake Hallie with my husband, an East Coast city kid, he sat at the kitchen counter with binoculars and a camera around his neck like some overzealous tourist, alternating between close-ups of the great blue heron or osprey and nature shots of muskrats or snapping turtles. Finally, I nailed a hook near the window so he could at least have his camera and binoculars within reach. He still screams for me whenever an eagle swoops down to fish. I didn't know as a teenager: everyone who moves here wants to stay forever.

Karen's mom, Helen, grew up on a Lake Hallie farm and moved into a house at the other end of the lake when she married. Though she's lived on water for more than eighty years, she never learned to swim. Helen's father owned nearly every parcel of land along Lake Hallie, and he ran the Hoot, a dance hall overlooking the lake. Between 1950 and 1964, many teens experienced their first dance or kiss or drink at the Hoot. Anyone who lived here back then has a story about the Hoot or its quirky proprietor, Karen's grandpa Clark Hughes. Kay, one of my university colleagues, remembers watching two young men fist fight in the Hoot's parking lot. When Clark stepped in to break up the fight, he intended to punch one of the scrapping guys but instead connected with Kay's face. Clark felt terrible, of course. Kay sported a pretty good shiner for the next few weeks; she told the story for the next six decades.

Old timers remember that Clark Hughes campaigned so ardently for John F. Kennedy that he was a guest at Kennedy's inaugural ball. Later, Hughes proposed that northern Wisconsin and Michigan's Upper Peninsula should break off to create a new state called Superior. His idea gained national publicity but—no surprise—not a lot of support. The Hoot closed over fifty years ago, but Clark Hughes's legacy lives on at the handicap-accessible boat landing that bears his name on land he donated.

The Hoot burned to the ground in 1978. Since Karen's grandpa owned the land, we partied around a bonfire at its concrete remains all through high school. On warm summer nights, Karen and I sat at what may have been the dance floor, talking and drinking, hearing occasional whoops from patrons at Slim's Saddle Bar across the highway. Karen and I imagined the ghosts of those teenagers who had the time of their lives on summer evenings many years ago, and we even sometimes felt them milling around the edges of our fire. As long as we were together, neither of us was ever afraid.

Man with Dog

The lone fisherman, in his red boat with his spotted English setter, glides along the water. There is nothing else to break its surface. Out my window is an L.L.Bean commercial: the brightness of the red boat on these blue waters, the perfect dog to take fishing.

It's too much of a cliché to say the lake on this early morning is like glass or a mirror, yet all of the clouds and trees are reflected on its surface so that if I were to photograph it at just this moment, a stranger would not be able to tell what is up or down, sky or water.

Lake Hallie is so narrow, from shore to shore, that my husband and I recognize the regulars who fish here, though we've never met them. My soldier son would say it's thirty meters across, and I would say it's the length of a basketball court. Our neighbors across the lake say we live "across the street." My husband is nearing seventy, but when we moved here years ago we became the new kids on this lake.

We call our frequent fishermen Handsome Man (a Robert Redford lookalike with a fancy boat) and Man Fishing with Wife (he baits the hooks for both of them; she wears a straw hat and complains) and Man with Dog (a gray-haired guy with a beautiful dog), the way a copywriter might label a new storyboard for an ad campaign. This morning, Man with Dog fly-fishes—smooth, easy throws like flicking a fine whip made of dental floss. His dog—always at the bow of the boat, always at attention—watches the lake. They float past me, and it's too heart-stopping to wave: the lake this early morning really is a mirror. Two men, two boats, two dogs. From my sliding glass doors, I know they cannot see this one woman watching.

Man with Dog wears a ball cap and a blue denim shirt. I can't see, but I would guess his collar is frayed. His dog has a long, regal face like a great-grandfather. The first year we lived here, I took their photograph from inside my house and later included it on a calendar I made for Bruce. Man with Dog is a stranger but a part of our lives. He has no idea.

Man with Dog trolls along the shore and casts. He turns off his motor to float back down the middle of the lake. He likes routines, as do I. *Who loves this man?* I find myself wondering. His dog, of course, but does he have a spouse? If I were married to Man with Dog, I would beg to come along on a morning like this. I concoct an entire life for him, beginning with the line "A widower and his dog."

He cannot know that every day I grow more in love with my aging husband. Nor that the sound of Bruce snoring while I do downward dog fills me with an overwhelming peace and warmth.

Man with Dog and I do not really know each other—to him I may be just Woman in the Window—but we know a few of the other's habits. This morning, I wave as he passes by. He waves back.

Living on Summer Time

A tiny Norwegian island north of the Arctic Circle, Sommarøy ("Summer Island"), recently made the news for its Let's Stop Time campaign to create the modern world's first time-free zone. Many of its 350 residents signed a petition to do away with clocks, deadlines, and closing times during its seventy days of around-the-clock sunshine this summer.

Lifelong resident Kjell Ove Hveding, whose family has been on the island since 1832, says, "Even after work, the clock takes up your time. People have forgotten how to be impulsive, to decide that the weather is good, the sun is shining, I can just live."

Amen to that. Even though I have ten days off from work, I can't sit still. I'm like a shark; if I stop moving, I'll die. Kayaking is the perfect solution: keep paddling and do nothing but look at Lake Hallie and enjoy what the Japanese call a "nature bath."

I have visited this lake since the summer I turned seven. Once when my best friend, Karen, and I were bobbing in front of her house—pushing off the sandy bottom and bursting out of the water—she pulled me up by the hair to save me from drowning. It wouldn't have been much of a story except, when Karen's mom brought me home, she told my mother. I would have just as soon left it between the Sabaskas and me.

Once we were alone, Mom scolded, "What would I have done

if you'd drowned?" I would not truly understand until I became a mother myself.

That night, I wrote to my older sister in Milwaukee and told her in detail about my new friend and what happened my first time at Karen's house. Juliann recently gave me back that 1975 letter, which captures in my loopy, just-learned cursive how much I've always loved Karen and Lake Hallie.

Back then, I remember thinking, *If I lived out here, I'd swim every day.* Now I've lived on Lake Hallie for almost a decade, and I've been swimming only once. My seven-year-old self would be appalled. The week of my fifty-first birthday, I paddle Lake Hallie. The mirrorlike water and the fluidity of time conspire to make thirty or forty years on this lake seem to pass in a few ripples.

At age eleven, summers were endless for Karen and me. Seeing each other when we were not in school was a rare treat. Even though we lived only six miles apart, arrangements had to be made and parents asked, unlike the daily bike rides we each made to visit different neighborhood friends.

At Karen's house, we swam and canoed. I liked exploring Lake Hallie, but each time Karen steered us to the middle, she stood up and rocked the boat until it tipped and filled with water. In I would go, one hand to my face to protect my thick glasses from sinking to the bottom.

Karen remembers it differently. Forty years later, she claims she dumped me only once. "But it was traumatic," I tease. How can we ever gauge the difference between what we remember and what really happened?

As eleven-year-olds at my house in Chippewa Falls, we slept in a Smokey travel trailer parked in the driveway—a mini-apartment for us. One night, Karen and I played cards at the tiny table. Before bedtime, we heard banging on the steel trailer. We looked at each other, eyes wide. Karen mouthed: "You know what

I'm gonna do? Get under the table." We both slid off the cushions and hid under the table that would soon fold out into our bed.

We trembled side by side, eyes flitting from window to locked door. Someone turned the doorknob. Just like in a horror movie, we were too stunned to scream. My heart jumped around inside my nightgown.

Then Dad's face appeared in the crank-out window: "What's going on in there?" He unlocked the door with his key and found us beneath the table. His giggling filled the camper. Karen and I let out relieved guffaws. Being scared is a part of childhood, but I don't recall ever feeling more petrified.

Karen and I are now the same age my dad was then. We will keep telling this story until we die.

At age twenty-one, Karen and I couldn't get enough summertime. We laid in the sun during the day, waitressed at night, and drank at Slim's, where old saddles topped the barstools. Sometimes we built bonfires at the cement ruins where her grandpa Clark Hughes's dance hall, the Hoot, once stood. We swam in his quarry ponds with sandy bottoms and beer-colored water, adjacent to Lake Hallie.

We were on the edge of our adult lives. Karen loved a boy she would eventually marry. At the end of summer, a boy I was seeing would tell me he wanted someone else. That day, I sat outside at Karen's house and sobbed in her arms. I gazed across Lake Hallie at a funky two-story cabin, one that resembled a wedding cake with a tier sliding slightly to one side. Back then, I could not have dreamed I would someday live there with my husband, Bruce, a man I didn't know I was just two weeks away from meeting. Back then, I could not imagine how happy I'd be.

Now, Karen lives in my childhood neighborhood and I'm in hers, the same six miles separating us. We talk on the phone each weekday morning while I drive to campus and she tools around highways in her dump truck. We see each other most weekends, usually for beer at my kitchen counter after she visits her mom, who is just yelling distance across Lake Hallie from me.

Turns out, Sommarøy's Let's Stop Time campaign was a public relations stunt to attract tourists. In the Chippewa Valley, we don't need months of midnight sun to take islander Hveding's advice: put away your watch while the sun is shining. Just live.

I'd like to say Karen and I kayak together often, but the last time was on my fiftieth birthday. I packed us Lake Hallie mojitos, and we toured the lake we've been paddling together for over forty years. Nothing exciting happened, and that's just the way we like it. Who knows what our future selves will look back on—perhaps the night a few years ago when we concocted plans for a zipline from her mom's house to mine. I hope my old graying self enjoys that ride.

Egg Laying

Often when I come home from work, my retired husband reports his daily news from Lake Hallie. Today he tells me about a teen fisherman who called out to him from a paddle boat as Bruce sat inside at our kitchen counter: "There's a chipmunk caught in your net."

Bruce walked down to the dock and saw a chipmunk struggling to untangle itself from a long-handled scoop net—something we keep for the big fish we never catch, more prop than function. Another chipmunk stood on the dock near his trapped pal. This is the influence of Chip 'n' Dale: can any of us look at chipmunks and not see them as naughty cartoons? Bruce, king of dad jokes, told the teen: "I wasn't even fishing for chipmunks."

Bruce held out the net, and the fisherman poked the snarl just enough for Chip to hop out and scurry under the dock with his buddy.

Animals on Lake Hallie thrill a city kid like Bruce. When we first moved here, he'd send me emails at work—"Otters playing on the lake" or "Great blue heron arrived this morning"—like headlines or invitations to come home that moment. Any given day, we may watch woodchucks, eagles, muskrat, and fox. I was once chased by a leaping mink and intimidated by a teeth-baring fisher, a weasel-like animal that kills porcupines by slashing their faces. Bruce is jealous that I've seen two coyotes and a lone timber wolf. After my second falcon sighting, he teased, "Today I saw a dinosaur and you didn't."

One Saturday in June, just past dawn, I open my curtains and notice what looks like a large hunk of black plastic in my yard. I do a double take—the plastic has a long neck. A snapping turtle. Her back legs are buried in the dirt, and I know at once: she's laying eggs.

I grab my camera. Bruce will want to see this, though not enough to wake up at five thirty in the morning. I watch as eggs the size of Ping-Pong balls drop from the back of this big girl into the shallow hole she's dug. Her shell is three feet from tip to tip, I confirm later when I measure the spot. She strains her body forward, one egg drops, and her large claws (the X-Men's Wolverine comes to mind) cover it with dirt. She produces another and another. I lose count after fifteen. Most snappers lay twenty to sixty eggs in one nest chamber. She lays each egg exactly the same way, yet I take photo after photo. I'll send some to my son, who is living in the desert and missing green Wisconsin. He's at officer's training, and we've had no contact for weeks. My mantra as a military parent: No news is good news.

When I was a brand-new mother, I read that the first lesson of parenthood is letting go. Holding my infant, how could I believe it? Little by little, we all have to. In a recent phenomenon called "helicopter parenting," moms and dads are so hyper-focused on their kids that they hover over their every move and decision, often tethered by cell phones, so that kids don't have the chance to function on their own. I know how important it is to let children experience not just skinned knees but also setbacks and failures, loss and heartbreak, in order to build their personal grit. I also know that urge to swoop in and save the day.

Turtles are a far cry from helicopter parents. This snapper lays eggs and leaves, then lets her babies' homing devices lead them to water.

Each June, near Lake Hallie (or any body of water in Wisconsin), we slow our cars for small painted turtles and enormous snappers crossing the road. We watch from afar as they dig nests in flower beds or gravel driveways. Bruce jokes that this is "e-reptile dysfunction," but who is to doubt 250 million years of turtle evolution? Somehow the species survives, even though 90 percent of snapper eggs are eaten by predators—skunks, chipmunks, raccoons, and great blue herons, to name a few. Watching this turtle—with its spiky carapace top shell and its prehistoric-looking legs and neck—feels like the closest I'll come to seeing a dinosaur.

Snappers have a terrible reputation for hunting swimmers, like some northern redneck version of *Jaws*, but they never attack while swimming and mostly want to be left alone. On land, snappers act more aggressively than other species because, unlike turtles with smaller bodies, they can't retreat inside their shell for safety. No option for flight means more fight.

Our snapper's nest chamber is close to the lake, so when these tiny turtles hatch, they will have an easy six-foot downhill tumble to water. Still, it's a terrible spot: not so close to my fire ring that the eggs will boil but near enough that I decide a bonfire is out of the question.

Bruce gets up around eight o'clock, and I show him a few photos as he drinks his morning coffee. Then I walk him to the upturned earth. He immediately goes to Facebook (where else?) to ask advice on how to protect our eggs. Within minutes come responses from sardonic writer types ("Are turtle eggs tasty in an omelet?"), no-nonsense environmental types ("Leave them alone and let nature take its course"), and helpful friends who advise to cover the area with a laundry basket, one with holes large enough to allow the hatchlings to escape but small enough to keep predators out.

Bruce retrieves an old basket from the garage. For the rest

of the summer, we work around the laundry basket, hoping the eggs are safe. Visitors joke about "Bruce's babies." I worry my lawnmower vibrations might damage them.

Come late September—almost 120 days after the egg laying—Bruce and I face the fact that none of this snapper's brood survived, part of the cruel world of nature. I lift off the basket and gingerly dig into the spot where I know the mama laid her eggs. Nothing is there. Not a partial shell nor an unhatched egg.

Parenting is so much more than laying eggs and walking away. Still, we can learn from reptiles how to let go, to trust in an instinct for water, to have a little faith that the universe may take care of us all.

Here We All Are

The Weinfurter family, circa 1934, including the author's mother (front row, second from left). COURTESY OF PATTI SEE

Forward

Throughout my life, I've called upon Wisconsin's state motto as my mantra in difficult times. "Forward" reminds us that things will get better.

Mottoes serve as states' mission statements, conveying in just a few words a reflection of their people or, more important, a hope. Consider Georgia's: "Wisdom, justice, moderation." Or other states with one-word maxims: New York's "Excelsior," Texas's "Friendship," Utah's "Industry." I love Hawaii's—"The life of the land is perpetuated in righteousness"—which sounds much more lyrical in native Hawaiian: *Ua Mau ke Ea o ka 'Āina i ka Pono*. I don't quite understand Oregon's—"She flies with her own wings"—though I appreciate its uplifting sentiment.

Turns out, "Forward" was not Wisconsin's first choice. Around 1850, our first governor, Nelson Dewey, asked University of Wisconsin Chancellor John Lathrop to design an official state seal. Lathrop depicted a scene inspired by Wisconsin Territory's motto: *Civilitas Successit Barbaruin* ("Civilization Succeeds Barbarism"). Story has it that when Dewey took the sketch to New York City to be cast in metal, he ran into a Milwaukee lawyer he knew named Edward Ryan. These two men discussed how neither of them liked Lathrop's pretentious motto. They sat down together on the steps of a Wall Street bank and held an impromptu meeting to brainstorm a phrase that would fit the plainspoken, hardworking people of their new state. They considered "Upward" and "Onward" before settling on "Forward," a reference to the resilience that still embodies Wisconsinites.

My parents and grandparents exemplified this grit. My mother's people, the Weinfurters, were a German farm family who settled in unincorporated Blenker, Wisconsin, in the 1880s. My grandfather was born on their farm in 1892, and my grandmother on a neighboring farm in 1896. Anna Altmann likely knew Ignatz Weinfurter for her entire life. They married at St. Kilian's, where all of their fifteen kids were baptized and one infant was buried. These Catholic farmers welcomed as many children as they could: gifts from God and cheap labor. As my own fifth-grade math problem, I figured out Anna was almost always pregnant for more than eleven years—longer than I'd been alive and for more than a quarter of her too-short life. She died of stomach cancer in 1938 when her youngest was a toddler and her oldest was twenty-four.

There is just one photograph of my mother with her family. I wonder what prompted that afternoon's pause from work? And who brought the camera, surely a luxury in the mid-1930s? Her parents sit in the middle, with children staged around them. A boy rests on Ignatz's lap; Anna is pregnant with baby number fifteen. The barn rises behind them, an icon of their past and future. My grandparents and their older kids survived World War I, the 1918 flu pandemic, and at the time of this picture, they had just come through the Great Depression. More tragedy was just around the corner.

Only one family photo was ever taken—something almost unimaginable in today's snap-happy world. As a kid, I gazed at this barnyard portrait and recalled the nursery rhyme: "There was an old woman who lived in a shoe. She had so many children, she didn't know what to do." I felt simultaneously sorry about their woes and pleased not to be these strange relatives. You can see their dirty faces and imagine their bare feet. Still, in the front row a curly-haired girl wearing a worn checkered dress smiles as if there's no reason not to. Fast-forward: she becomes my mother.

Ignatz always loved beer, and once Anna was gone, his drinking increased. During his worst benders, he lived in the shed and the older girls brought him meals. His kids who still lived at home took care of one another, and his two married daughters checked in when they could. One day, without warning, Ignatz gave away his fourteen-year-old daughter to another farm family. Who knows what sort of deal was made. From then on, whenever nuns from St. Kilian's came to visit the Weinfurter farm, my fearful mother hid in the barn so she would not be the next child given up. She was eight years old.

The girl who was handed over, not unlike a runt-of-the-litter piglet, did not speak of it until she was eighty-something. I interviewed her for a family oral history project as my mom became more and more lost in an Alzheimer's haze. At the mention of Ignatz's name, my aunt clammed up like the rejected teenager she once was. "I'm not going to talk about him," she seethed. She recalled that she cried every day until her new family simply gave her back. Such trauma festers, becoming a bruise that stains forever. Still, for this child tested by poverty and loss, the only option was forward.

Two years after Anna's death, a drunken Ignatz was dropped off at home by a friend one April night and, as he crossed the highway, was run over by a young man he'd been with at the tavern. The Weinfurter children watched as their father's broken body was pulled from the ditch in front of their farmhouse. He died of massive head injuries. This was big news for papers in Marshfield and Wisconsin Rapids, the closest cities. The headline "Car Fatally Injures Farmer in Front of Home" made it as far as the *Capital Times* in Madison.

A coroner's inquest determined that a dark figure on a dark highway after midnight was an accident waiting to happen. The Weinfurters forgave that drunk driver—Clarence, a boy they all knew—and simply carried on. It was 1940. Two years later, he served in the Pacific Theater during World War II. Clarence's idea of forward took him far away, then back home again to raise a family. He died at age ninety-two.

I did not know this story until my father handed me Clarence's obituary in 2012 and said simply, "He killed your grandfather." Turns out, my parents kept tabs on this man from afar, a lesson in how forgiveness does not always mean erasing the past.

Over one hundred years after the two Blenker farm kids fell in love, Ignatz and Anna have nearly one thousand descendants scattered around the United States. The word *forward* likely never crossed my grandparents' lips. Yet here we are. Here we all are.

Joyful Mysteries

My mom is in the hospital for observation following a series of ministrokes. She did not want to go out like this: after she was diagnosed with Alzheimer's nine years ago, she said she never wanted to burden her family or have a life in which she couldn't do what she liked.

I sit close to her bed and flip through TV channels. I settle on *Terminator 2*—not so dramatic on this tiny TV mounted in the far corner of the room. My mom hasn't been able to follow a storyline for about seven years now. Still, she understands the universal language of blowing shit up.

"Wow," she says periodically throughout Arnold Schwarzenegger's shootout sequences.

A cardiac sonographer wheels his portable echocardiogram machine into the room and asks, "Is now a good time?" I mute the TV, and he attaches his round sticky pads to my mom's chest, careful to never expose either breast. He talks to Mom about what he's doing.

"She can't really communicate anymore," I tell him.

Still, he says to her, "This echo will tell us if your heart is damaged."

She keeps her eyes on me and smiles. On the small monitor, this grainy slug of my mother's heart looks like a gray hand flipping a middle finger with each quick beat. My eyes well up as I watch in awe. Many of us have seen an ultrasound of our own unborn babies, but few have the opportunity to view a parent's beating heart.

"Everything looks just fine," the sonographer says. I cry some more. She could linger like this for many years. Alzheimer's teaches us there are possibilities worse than death.

Mom can no longer walk on her own, and we know that eventually she will lose the ability to smile, to swallow, to speak. This prompted me to record my parents' voices starting a few years earlier. I held my MP3 player in my hand, hoping its small size meant that my recording session would be more like a casual visit than an awkward interview. Though I had prepared questions to ask my dad ("What were your jobs on the farm as a kid?" and "What surprised you about the way your life turned out?"), mostly my recordings were daily adventures of an octogenarian couple and their adult daughter. On one, I'm mixing cookie batter, narrating as I stir, while Mom has a conversation with the button on her sweater and Dad reads the grocery store flyer aloud to us. On another, Mom sings along with a Christmas album. She doesn't know her own name, but she can sing "Adeste Fidelis" entirely in Latin. Today in the hospital, I contemplate that I may never hear my mother speak a coherent sentence again.

After the sonographer wheels away his equipment, the breakfast tray arrives, and I coax Mom into eating a few bites of waffle. I narrate just as I do with her at home: "Look: syrup in a little square container. You like syrup."

She doesn't know what to do with the straw in her mouth, and she has trouble swallowing. Finally, I give up feeding her and flip through channels.

I stop when I get to the nuns. Mom perks up as soon as she sees them. We join the rosary in progress, in the midst of the Joyful Mysteries. The nuns are in full regalia, and for a moment

I can't think of what their outfits are called. I might have twelve years of Catholic school behind me, but today I'm functioning on too little sleep. My mind is murky.

Mom hasn't spoken much beyond "wow" in almost twenty-four hours. Now she says the prayers with these church-channel nuns, as real to her as if they were in the same room with us. She says the Apostles' Creed, Our Father, Hail Mary, Glory Be. She knows every word.

Mom fingers the edge of her blankets, I suspect looking for her rosary beads. All of her life, she prayed the rosary in bed, in her living-room rocker, at the kitchen table. She believed praying the rosary kept our car from a head-on collision on road trips and that every pregnancy—her own eight and her children's sixteen—produced a healthy child because of her daily devotions. "I never lost a one," she often said to me. She put her entire life in the hands of God, and she found comfort in the power of her rosary.

Now, the more prayers she says, the louder her voice becomes. I hold her hand. So much amazes: her strong heart, her stronger faith, these lessons she still continues to teach me.

"Habit," I say out loud to my mother. "Look, they're in their full habits."

One Saturday, months before Mom's ministrokes brought her to the hospital, I was recording our conversation while her big band album played in the background. She broke into song: "It's been a wrong, wrong time."

I said, "I think it's 'long, long time.'" We'd listened to this album every Saturday for almost three years. I would give her a bath after breakfast, and then we'd put on music in the living room until naptime.

She belted out, "Lick me once, and lick me twice, and lick me once again."

I burst into laughter. "It's 'kiss,' you goof." I giggled some more. "Kitty Kallen couldn't sing 'lick me' on the radio in 1945."

"They can get licks in there, too," she argued. "Some of the kids do that." She kept singing, "Kiss me once, and kiss me twice, then kiss me once again. It's been a long, long time."

"I bet you were quite the kisser," I said.

"Uh-huh. I love it."

I laughed until I cried. A daughter's joy. A mother's mystery.

A Brief Story

One Saturday morning, I visit my dad, and he's got piles of men's white briefs on his kitchen table. He tells me he's been to his neighbor's thrift sale where he bought twenty-eight pairs of "undershorts" for five dollars.

Pete died a few weeks ago at age eighty-nine, and his children have been holding a sale at his house for the last three days. Dad took many trips around the corner: on the first day to see what goods were displayed in Pete's driveway and to catch up with Pete's kids, and then on subsequent days to see how much their prices had come down.

As long as I can remember, my parents loved lingering at thrift sales and looking through tables of other people's junk. They saw not just an acquaintance's butter dish or half-finished hook rug but a treasure with a history, often for the right price. Mom and Dad grew up in farm families and survived the Great Depression. Mom was the eleventh of fifteen children; Dad was one of four. Neither of them had anything but secondhand (or third- or fourth-) clothes and toys until they started working and could buy items themselves. Then they had their first seven kids in twelve years, and any desire to buy something new was put on hold. Still, their motto could have been "nothing you asked for and more than you wanted."

When Mom got too sick to join Dad on their thrift-sale

adventures, he rarely left the house except for church and the grocery store. Last month, Mom moved into an Alzheimer's unit, which means not only has Dad been able to play cribbage at a bar on Saturday afternoons, but he has also resumed his weekly trips to shop for junk.

～

One summer afternoon in 1972, when I was four, neighbor Pete was the hero who carried me home in his arms after a bike accident. Mom and Dad were gone for the day, and my sister Geralynn—a few months away from starting high school—must have been in charge of my brother David and me. We were the youngest three of eight kids. My parents finally could relax after years of crowd control; they raised all of us in a one-and-a-half story home with one bathroom.

We were allowed to do pretty much anything, as long as we didn't leave the yard. Geralynn could climb a rickety wooden ladder to sunbathe on the flat, tar-papered garage roof, baby oil puddled in her belly button, and smoke Kools up there with her two best friends, Sue and Barb, whose houses were on either side of ours. Even at eleven, David could back the mammoth station wagon out of the driveway and park it on the street if he had friends over to play basketball. I could turn on the oven and make myself an open-faced toasted cheese under the broiler at four years old. Just as long as we stayed in the house or yard.

That July day, Mom and Dad left us with one familiar rule. Mom told us individually and then yelled it out the car window as Dad accelerated: "Don't leave the yard." Geralynn, David, and I stood in the driveway and waved goodbye.

Forty-some years later, David told me, "It was a day sort of like today: blue skies, just perfect weather." Of course we weren't going to stay in the yard. I often rode on the handlebars of his bike or Geralynn's, even though Mom told me not to. Their bikes were his and hers versions of the same model—David's was mustard brown with a high, straight "boy bar" connecting seat to handlebars, and Geralynn's was turquoise with a low "sissy bar," as we called crossbars—both with banana seats, tall chrome backrests, and high monkey handlebars. David recalls that Dad took them to the Super America, back then a mini-department store. They both got to pick out a brand new Schwinn—quite a milestone considering that they rarely had new clothes, much less new bicycles.

I don't remember, but I'm guessing there were Old Maid cards clothes-pinned to the spokes of one of the bikes on the day of our accident. I know for sure they were there when I inherited Geralynn's bike two years later, after I finally learned to ride and she passed her driver's test.

At four years old, I couldn't verbalize what the world looked like from the handlebars of an older sibling's bike, but I knew it was a taste of what was to come: the freedom to ride away from home and the possibility to just keep pedaling and see where it would take me. Surely, many kids' fantasies about adulthood begin on a bike.

I don't remember the accident. Maybe I wiggled at the exact moment when David made a turn into the alley by Pete's driveway. His wheel twisted sharply, I slid off the handlebars, and my small bare foot thrust into the spokes of his spinning front wheel. We both tumbled to the ground. I have some shadow memory of lying in the alley and screaming, and then of Pete swooping me up and carrying me to my home one block away, blood dripping off my foot. I also remember sitting on the edge of the bathtub while David coaxed me to dip my bloody foot into the cool water. My wound may not have been more than a scrape, but I was limping when Mom and Dad came home from the bar hours later.

I always wondered if Pete told them what happened. Was this a story he recapped to his wife and kids? I walked past his house daily on my way to and from Holy Ghost Grade School.

I sometimes pondered the name on his mailbox: M. Pete Sabin. What did the *M* stand for? Melvin? Marvin? Murgatroyd? Mystery Pete Sabin. I wondered if Pete ever caught a glimpse of me walking or riding my bike, or if he ever saw my picture in the local paper for some sports award and thought, "There's the little girl I carried home."

I've never known if my parents thanked Pete for helping us.

Mom and Dad have owned a home in this neighborhood since 1953. Now that Pete is dead, my dad has lived here longer than anyone else on the block. Today, Dad has twenty-eight pairs of Pete's underwear on his kitchen table.

Dad has always slept in just his underwear—even during Wisconsin winters—and he used to walk around the house in them briefly each morning and night. The same goes for my two older brothers. All three guys in our house lounged around in what I learned to call tighty-whities in high school. This is one of those innocent scenarios that only seems weird when I look back at it, much like sharing bathwater with seven older siblings. The youngest would go first, and each older kid got to add a little more hot water. Viewing these memories through the lens of today's standards, they warrant an emphatic *eww*.

Today I say to Dad, "Just make sure you wash Pete's underwear."

He says, "They all fit but two pairs, so I gave those to Justin next door."

"Nooo." I say it a little too forcefully.

Dad stares at me. "What? He'll wear them."

I can't imagine that my dad's forty-something neighbor, a corrections officer at the local prison, would welcome anybody's preowned tighty-whities. I'm sure he was sweet to Dad, a kind, goofy octogenarian next door who waves across the hedge and shares a Leinenkugel's once in a while. But I doubt Justin would speak the word *underwear* aloud in Dad's presence, much less accept them as a gift.

⌒

Often, when neighbors die, I discover from their obituaries that they were so much more than the folks I thought I knew. Pete's featured something that always draws me in: young and old photographs of the deceased. I think of them as before and after pictures.

"Before Pete" was a beautiful young man (a boy!) in his white silk pilot's scarf and bombardier's hat with goggles atop his head. He flew a B-17 Flying Fortress and was shot down over France. A little research turns up our local newspaper's report that on July 8, 1943, Pete's mother received this news in a War Department telegraph, and for eight weeks she waited for more information about her missing-in-action son.

As the mother of a soldier myself, I cannot fathom what those fifty-six days were like for her. Finally, another telegram arrived: "Am pleased to inform you your son returned to duty September 7." Pete was awarded an Air Medal for "courage, skill, and coolness in the line of duty," and a few weeks later, he telephoned his mom, though he could not mention where he'd been for those lost two months. We live in a small town. This was big news in 1943; but even seventy-plus years later, and in the midst of another war, anyone's son going missing in action would still be news in the *Chippewa Herald*.

"After Pete" appears as the old dude I knew, one who worked as a rural letter carrier, raised two children with his wife, tended his garden, and drove his motor-scooter to the tavern for happy hour. Every time I saw him after my bike accident in 1972, I thought, "That's the guy who carried me home." I didn't pay attention to anything else about him.

Now I know Pete's given name was Myron. He was a war hero, and he wore white briefs, just like my dad.

Fine Music

Sometimes I drive my husband's new MINI Cooper to work, the fancy car with a radio neither of us has been able to figure out how to set. I mindlessly seek stations down Highway 53. This morning, I settle on WCFW out of Chippewa Falls—the station I was forced to listen to as a kid.

My mother's morning ritual included opening the mustard-colored curtains in our dining room and turning on her square, black radio balanced on the windowsill. Its antenna was angled toward the East Hill where WCFW's small tower shot above two-story homes. Decades later, the station's slogan endures—"Where FM means fine music"—and it is still the only family-owned station in the Chippewa Valley.

WCFW went on air in 1968, just three months after I was born. Every morning of my childhood began with the "Too Fat Polka" or "Beer Barrel Polka" or "In Heaven There Is No Beer"—songs many Wisconsin kids can name. I knew Whoopee John and the Six Fat Dutchmen by ear. My mom could sing every song.

Every morning, from five-thirty to eight, was polka time, and that's still true. I swear the same deejay from my childhood is still on: I wouldn't forget his slightly whistled S's, surely caused by dentures.

We've all heard reports of soon-to-be mothers putting head-phones over their bulging bellies and piping in Beethoven or

Mozart in an attempt to increase their babies' intelligence and well-being. My brain during infancy, toddlerhood, childhood, and adolescence was wired to the Chmielewski brothers or Lawrence Welk. All of this may account for my inability to sit down and relax as an adult.

In 1981, MTV was born. Sometime in high school, I started eating my morning Wheaties in front of the living room television, where "Video Killed the Radio Star" drowned out "Let Me Call You Sweetheart" spilling from my mom's radio a room away. After that, my life was filled with more Weird Al Yankovic than Polka King Frankie Yankovic, and I paid attention to polkas only at an occasional wedding when the deejay went old school.

Decades later, when my mom didn't recognize her husband or kids or grandkids or even her own name, she still tapped a toe when she heard a song she liked. Scientists have long known that music is hardwired into the brain's right hemisphere, a means of communication when words fail. And so it was for my mother in late-stage Alzheimer's, what the poet Anne Sexton wrote about in "Music Swims Back to Me": "In a funny way / music sees more than I. / I mean it remembers better." Even when Mom began losing her ability to speak, she could still sing lyrics learned seventy years earlier—often a polka.

∽

Music is memory, and listening to WCFW this morning, I remember that on some of those polka mornings of my childhood, my mom's nightgown was on inside out or backwards, or both. When I would point this out, she'd laugh and tell us, "That's what happens when I get changed in the dark." My dad was up and out the door by five each morning to get to his job on the Soo Line Railroad, and he went to bed sometimes before us kids. Mom was a night owl, perhaps from her years of staying up to bake and mend and clean once all of her eight kids went to bed. Getting up early to send her last two kids, David and me, off to school was probably a struggle. She started each day with a cup of coffee and a cigarette from her Tupperware pouch—hard plastic for her pack of Lucky Strikes, front slot for a book of matches—oblivious that her clothes were in disarray as she set a box of Shredded Wheat on the table.

Even at the time, I wondered why her nightgown was only sometimes on backwards, though Mom was the woman who once went to church with yesterday's girdle and nylons caught in a flare leg of her pants. Just before communion, she crossed her legs and a bit of the nylons peeked out between her hem and her shoe. She gave them a good pull and discreetly put the snarl of nylons and girdle in her purse. When she got home, she laughed till she cried, unable to get the words out. She just stood in the kitchen, holding the stretchy nest and motioning to her blue pumps.

Twenty years later, I was a young mother slipping back into my nightgown in the dark when I had an epiphany about my mom. That weekend, I told my older brother, David: "I think Mom's nightgown was inside out because she put it on after sex."

We were at a supper club bar with our spouses—all of us in our thirties. After many cocktails, it made sense to solve that long-standing mystery. Why else would I use the words *sex* and *Mom* in the same sentence?

"No," David responded quickly. "She said she got dressed in the dark."

"That was her story," I told him.

"How do you know?"

"I just do."

We leave it at that.

I won't explain to anyone that as I get older, I find more and more connections between my mother and me, ones my teenage self would be mortified to hear. I love listening to polkas. And I wear my nightgown whichever way I please.

Tonight at Dad's

My seven siblings and I meet at our parents' house to prep a photo board for Mom's funeral tomorrow. After supper, my brother David brings out old home movies that he has recently transferred from VHS to DVD, a process that seems something like converting a walkie-talkie into a smartphone. We gather in the living room and travel fourteen years into the past as we watch our parents open gifts at their fiftieth wedding anniversary.

Mom's voice is almost shrill, or so it seems to me now. Alzheimer's silenced her. After my parents open their gifts, Mom forces her large foot into the tiny open-toed wedding shoes she wore in 1948 when she was eighteen. Behind them hang her wedding dress and Dad's suit, which David suspended from the ceiling as decorations.

"I'm Cinda—" Mom says on the video. She can't quite get the words out over her laughter. "Cinda—" she tries to say, "—rella!" She laughs some more.

Tonight at Dad's, we all sit here transfixed by Mom on the screen. She hadn't been able to sit up or smile for months before she died; she hadn't recognized any of us kids for years.

Dad says now, "I must have had a cold." He's in his lift chair, an oversized recliner with an electric motor that allows him to easily get his eighty-six-year-old body in and out of it; I'm sitting on the floor at his feet because we've got twenty family members packed into this small living room to watch David's videos.

"You were crying," I say over my shoulder. We all watch him on the screen, as he hands his tissue to Mom. She takes off her glasses and wipes her eyes. She's crying from laughing so hard; he's crying because he is what Mom always called a softie. I don't have to look behind me right now to know he's leaking tears again.

~

Sometimes home videos contain ordinary moments or milestones that were meant to be viewed at a future date. Sometimes they are love letters from the past, opened when we most need them.

The next video shows Christmas Eve at David's house. Our parents are there, delivering their traditional red garbage bag full of gifts to his four little ones. David's youngest, Evin, unwraps a jogging suit from his grandparents, then strips to his socks and underwear and puts on his new clothes. We roar with laughter, but the people in the video don't even seem to notice. Evin runs a wide lap around the room as David records, the four-year-old body blurring out of the frame and then back in.

"Dad," Evin yells, "Dad, I got a jogging suit, so I'm jogging."

My mom tells Evin's brother to stop it when he tries to interrupt Evin's jog. Her sharp tone is one my siblings and I all recognize. We sit together in Dad's living room while our mother is being prepared at the funeral home three miles away, and each of us does an impression of Mom's other go-to phrases. "Shame on you." "Is that what you learned in school?" "Son of a buck."

Tomorrow we'll see Mom for the last time, in her casket. Tonight we watch her on the TV screen because of a treasure David brought for us in his coat pocket. I'm not sad, tonight at Dad's, where the idea of personal space disintegrates when we all pack in.

Sometimes on Christmas, all these bodies make the house feel claustrophobic. The warm air can get so thick, we open the front and back doors. But tonight it feels good, close, just what I need.

I sit on the carpeted floor with my nieces, all in their twenties, though on the screen they are little girls in bib overalls and big glasses. Four of my sisters squeeze onto Dad's couch. Another leans against a paneled wall. And the guys stand around tonight at Dad's—one hand in a jeans pocket, one hand wrapped around a beer—just like they do in the video.

Mourning Portrait

The night before Mom's funeral, after gathering with my family, I sit at my kitchen counter drinking and listening to audio recordings I made before she stopped speaking a year ago. Each time I recorded Mom and Dad, I'd come home and listen, usually like this, late at night.

Mom died on Thursday, and now it's Sunday. These past four weeks, I haven't gone a day without seeing her. Tomorrow I'll touch my mother for the last time. I can't wrap my mind around that, so I sit at the counter and let her voice fill my kitchen. This is my wake.

Years ago, Dad decided that we should offer a two-hour visitation before Mom's funeral when the day came, so everything would happen in one day. "Not enough tears for two days," he chuckled, using his humor to acknowledge how exhausting it would be to mourn and greet the public at his age.

Traditionally, a wake was held the night before a funeral, allowing people to view the body of a loved one and keep watch over it, usually at home. In some cultures, a wake allowed time to make sure the person was truly dead. Sometimes a bell was attached to the body with string so a family member would hear if the person stirred.

Mom once told me the most afraid she'd ever been as a child

was when her parents were laid out in their coffins in the family living room in 1938 and 1940. She was eight years old for the first death and ten for the second. I never asked if Mom lay in bed with her sisters those nights, listening for the tinkling of the bell that would mean her parents' untimely deaths—cancer and a car accident—had been horrific mistakes.

As a child, I found coffin photos of my grandparents in our attic, keepsakes Mom could not part with, though she would never display them. She owned just one other photo of her parents, a wedding portrait. I remember taking sidelong glances at the dead bodies. Though I didn't know the word then, only one fits: *macabre*.

When I leave my house the morning of Mom's funeral, I pass Slim's Lake Hallie Tavern, where the barstools used to be topped with real saddles until some drunk fell off and sued. Even before nine o'clock, there's a group on the front porch smoking cigarettes. They are just off the eleven-to-seven shift, I'd guess, and drinking before bed. No one knows I'm on the way to my mother's funeral; it's just another Monday to the rest of the world.

In the church vestibule, I gather with Dad and my seven siblings, along with their spouses, children, and grandchildren.

"I've got Mom's purse with me today," I say to my sister. I hold it up.

"I'm wearing her dress," another sister says. A lovely navy blue print from 1950 or so, when Mom was a size five.

"I'm wearing her earrings," says another. These are sweet tributes, part of our own ceremony, though none of us had told the others our plans.

"I'm not wearing her underwear," a sister says. We all laugh. Dad divvied up Mom's granny panties to a few of us when she went into the nursing home fourteen months ago.

My son and his cousins go out to the hearse to get their

grandma. Last night, we estimated the weight: if Mom is 80 pounds and the casket is 220, then six grandkids can surely lift 50 pounds each.

When they carry her in, one of my sisters says, "Well, there she is," as if Mom's been missing. The pallbearers rest the casket on a cart and push Mom up to the altar. The undertakers, the Horan brothers, open her casket for our family viewing. This is the moment I have dreaded: seeing her laid out. Her casket seems too small to hold a body. My hands feel enormous. Everything is slightly fuzzy around the edges. For a moment, I think I might pass out.

I stand next to Dad. I hear one of my brothers suck in his breath and walk away. We've got about thirty minutes with Mom until guests start to arrive. *Let's just get through this* is all I can think.

"She's pretty," I say to no one in particular.

Dad didn't want anyone to photograph Mom during her last two weeks of life, given the absence of dentures and her empty stare. Today, she is beautiful. Anyone who knows her knows this isn't how she really looked, but she is lovely. The Horan brothers have filled in her cheeks—no longer the hollowed-out features of someone who forgot how to swallow—and they've given her back her large bust.

"Who brought a camera?" Dad asks.

"I did," I tell him.

He says, "Now you can take her picture."

Secret Spaces

"Wake up," I whispered into my sister Julie's sleepy face. "Let's make blueberry muffins." She was home for the weekend, and I was nestled between her and fourteen-year-old Geralynn early on a Saturday morning. As the youngest, I simply floated from bedroom to bedroom—passed around like a spinster aunt. I wouldn't get my own bed until I started kindergarten in the fall.

After my many tearful pleas for an Easy-Bake Oven, Mom finally said, exasperated, "You really want to cook with a lightbulb?! Just use the real oven." Thus began my love of baking.

Julie was seventeen and living with our twenty-four-year-old eldest sister ninety miles away. She was a kid herself, though it didn't seem so in 1973, when teens could smoke in front of their parents and go to bars or to war or to protests. Julie graduated from high school and—though no one knew it then—left home to become a hippie. She worked as a nurse aide and told us stories about her patients on every visit. She called me Margaret Muffin; I called her Thelma—after the two oddest women she cared for. She baked with me whenever I asked.

I wanted to be a baker; instead I became a writer.

Many years later, I read that during her lifetime, Emily Dickinson was better known for her baked goods than her poetry. Mount Holyoke Professor Christopher Benfey says, "In the kitchen, in the bedroom, these secret spaces where she could be alone . . . , that was really freedom. When Emily Dickinson bakes bread there's something almost ecstatic about it, satisfaction of creativity."

That's what I felt but could not yet convey at nearly five years old, stirring my batter as Julie looked on. And as we peered inside the oven to see if our muffins were rising. And as we set them, golden-topped, on the counter for the rest of our huge family to admire for a full second before they devoured every crumb. There's something primal about feeding the ones you love.

Mom baked everything with love. A cliché, I know, but she and Dad raised eight kids on a railroad worker's salary. Her inexpensive goodies were both sustenance and a carefully crafted treat for each of us. Joey loved angel food cake. David, ice cream Jell-O. Geralynn, dark chocolate cake. Julie and I, blueberry muffins. Sharon, Jackie, Mary? I can't recall, but Mom knew.

My earliest memories of Holy Ghost Grade School aren't of the classroom but of walking home, past the final turn into the alley that cut our block in half, and through our hedge until the aroma of Mom's cookies or muffins pulled me across our backyard. Mom's baking was perfectly planned so when we barreled through the back door, her sweets were cooling on the kitchen table. As a mother myself, I recognize it wasn't what she made that was so special but why and how she made it.

When Mom stirred cake batter, her whole body shook. She made it look like a workout—a word we wouldn't have used back then—and she made it fun.

The first time I baked Emily Dickinson's gingerbread recipe was for my dad just after Mom died. I consoled Dad with comfort food—baked treats and homemade soups—and as I cooked some of Mom's recipes in my own tiny kitchen, I comforted myself. Dad also started to bake, pies mostly, like his mother used to make.

The first Christmas without Mom, I gave Dad an apron. On

the front was a silkscreen photo of him and Mom on their sixty-fourth wedding anniversary. That day, she was lost in an Alzheimer's haze, but she still knew what to do when we brought out the camera: grasp her beloved's arm and smile wide.

I made an apron for Julie, too, with a blown-up photo of one of Mom's letters to her—filled with family news just after Julie moved out. A handwritten recipe might have been more appropriate on an apron, but Mom rarely had to write hers down.

Somebody Had to Do It

The author (third from left) with her family and friends at Jump River
Rosie's in 1976. PHOTO BY DAN GOULET

Tavern Tour

Visitors who come to Wisconsin are often amazed at the number of taverns. Whenever I travel, across state lines or across an ocean, I'm struck by the lack of them. I recently stayed thirty-five days in Zhuhai, China, and I spent the first week looking for a bar. We finally found Ryan's Place, run by a three-hundred-pound goatee-sporting Canadian who models his business after that other famous expatriate bar, Rick's Place. Ryan's no Humphrey Bogart, and Zhuhai is no Casablanca. Still, a couple of travelers from the Chippewa Valley settled in at the bar, and Matilda—the Mongolian barmaid—served us frosty glasses of Tiger Beer, complained about her boss, and asked my advice on how she should turn down drunken American men. Just like at home.

I'm a child of the 1970s and 1980s who grew up going to family taverns and supper clubs with my parents and siblings. I get nostalgic over the scent of Pine-Sol mixed with cigarette smoke and perfume, and over a jukebox playing "Good Hearted Woman" or "Mammas Don't Let Your Babies Grow Up to Be Cowboys."

Today, if parents took their kids to a bar that didn't serve food, social services would show up. But back then, in a small town like Chippewa Falls, it was perfectly acceptable for many parents—especially German American ones like mine—to include their children in tavern life. We'd take a Sunday afternoon drive and stop at a bar on the way home.

The supper clubs of my youth still prompt soothing thoughts: dark-paneled walls; tin beer signs (Leinenkugel's and Hamm's "from the Land of Sky Blue Waters," and none of them lit up); relish trays of celery, carrots, radishes, and a communal dip; bread baskets with white rolls and crackers wrapped in plastic and pats of butter; fried fish on Friday nights and prime rib on Saturdays; and waitresses in polyester dresses who greeted each table with: "How are youse guys?" At the bar before dinner, Dad might have had a brandy old-fashioned and Mom a Mogen David mixed with Sprite (never called a "wine spritzer"). Afterward, we'd go back to the bar for Mom's and Dad's pink squirrels or grasshoppers made with Olson's Creamland Dairy ice cream, and the kids would beg for a sip.

Since the colonial period, taverns have influenced the growth of American towns. For nearly a century, they offered one of the only other social outlets besides church. Wisconsin still has more bars per capita than any other state, a tradition that began when hundreds of German breweries started appearing in small towns in the mid- to late 1800s. These became what one historian calls "nerve centers," where townsfolk gathered for weddings and wakes or simply weekly parties.

Finding a watering hole is part of our heritage, since almost 43 percent of the state's current population descends from German roots. Germans call the comfort found in a family tavern *gemütlichkeit*. Its closest English translation is "coziness," a warmth referenced in many Wisconsin tavern names: the Laff-A-Lot Dance Hall, Happy Jack's, the Jolly Farmer Bar, the Welcome Matt. These are clubs not in the New York City sense of the word but in the VFW sense. Even the most recent Eau Claire–Chippewa Falls area phonebook lists them as taverns, not bars or clubs.

For a period of my life, I tried to deny where I came from. When my son's grandparents cared for him while his dad and I worked, I felt compelled to remind them, "Please don't take the baby to the bar." Now I realize their bar (was it Pretzel's then, or the Fill Inn?) was where all of their friends were, and they wanted to show off their first grandson. As Alex got older, they took him to supper clubs for dinner, letting him spin on a barstool and drink a Shirley Temple with a cocktail straw. Typical Wisconsin kid stuff.

For better or worse, mine is the last generation to grow up in the family tavern. Along the way, I learned 1) how to play darts, pool, and pinball, 2) how to talk to just about anyone, 3) that some folks go the bar because they don't want to go home, 4) that nobody likes a drunk, and 5) that hard drinking and smoking make you an old woman quickly.

⌒

Turning forty years old was a milestone that I didn't want to commemorate with black balloons and a cake in the shape of a male body part. Instead, my best friend, Karen, suggested we visit some of the taverns of our youth. As we wrote down our old haunts, we had a story or two about each, mostly tales we'd never tell our mothers or our teenage children.

Karen's a former bartender and waitress, someone who knows both sides of the bar. Tavern connoisseur? More like what the authors of *Badger Bars & Tavern Tales: An Illustrated History of Wisconsin Saloons* would call your "Basic Badger Barfly." In Chippewa Falls, we'd leave out *basic* and *badger*.

During the weeks surrounding my fortieth birthday, Karen and I stop at a series of places we'd been known to visit on one night of barhopping. First is Glen Loch Saloon (Bugeye's to locals), just past Irvine Park and near Glen Loch Dam. Tom "Bugeye" Stary, his gal Chris, and her kids have run the place for over twenty-seven years. The first time I went there as an adult, feeling brave and thirsty after spending the afternoon swimming in the river above the dam, I offered my driver's license to Bugeye even though I wasn't yet of legal drinking age. He thought it was cool that we shared the same birthday, July fourteenth. He told me to come back when I was twenty-one and he'd buy me a drink. A year later, I did.

Our next two stops happen the following week with a carful of friends. After our pre-tour dinner of grilled bratwurst, we get to Tip Top around eight o'clock on a Saturday night, just in time to see a wedding party come in. The bridesmaids and groomsmen stagger past in a sort of reverse receiving line, with tuxedo jackets off, bow ties lost, and fancy up-dos all but down. I'm reminded of another reason I've always loved bars—the people-watching.

Tip Top is one of the few neighborhood bars left in Chippewa Falls, just down the street from Notre Dame church and surrounded by hundred-year-old houses. Except for the lighted Leinenkugel's signs in the windows, a stranger might think this is just another house on the block. Inside the front door is a health department poster with a Lyme disease warning and pictures of various ticks.

When our driver orders a nonalcoholic beer, the tattooed bartender tells me she has to make a call to find one. I tell her not to worry and order him a Diet Coke.

We watch as a bridesmaid's crinoline layers stick to her barstool as she gets up and she drags the stool with her. We laugh and laugh.

"What else do you have hiding under there?" I tease her.

She hikes up her strapless gown and tells me, "The last time I was here, there was a reward sign for the return of a stolen barstool."

Our next stop is Loopy's Grill and Saloon on business Highway 29 just outside of Chippewa Falls. This was the Yellow Rose in the late 1980s and run by a family with two teenage daughters who sometimes bartended in the afternoons. Karen and I stopped weekly to play the jukebox ("Paradise by the Dashboard Light" may still be the only song I can sing beginning to end) and talk with the sisters, who always had a story or two. They couldn't have been more than fifteen and sixteen then, but they'd seen enough in their bar that they seemed much older to us.

The last time I visited, when I was twenty-two, the bar was full of bandana-wearing bikers and chain-smoking barflies having the time of their lives. I was one of them. Now, in addition to flat-screen satellite TVs on every wall, Loopy's offers outdoor deck seating and tube, kayak, and canoe rentals for the Chippewa River. There's even a fine-dining menu.

In the parking lot, I notice two vanity plates, TOP DAD and PEACHS, that tell me everything I need to know about Loopy's new clientele. A class reunion rages out back near the sand volleyball courts, and folks with peel-off name tags mill around a bonfire. Inside, others sing old karaoke songs popular in the mid-1990s. Some tipsy alum croons an off-key "My Heart Will Go On" with the same fervor I felt when I used to sing Meatloaf tunes at the top of my lungs, sometimes so loudly I drowned out the jukebox.

Clearly, this is no longer the roughneck bar I once knew. Still, some things about bar patrons never change: the courage we feel belting out songs we love, our delight at being together with friends, and the revelry that can only occur in our favorite taverns.

Why I Revere My Septic Guy

Historians claim the cornerstone of civilization is language. Other experts say it's religion, science, or even the family unit. I suggest something most of us do not consider: indoor plumbing.

I was at work when I noticed a text from my husband, Bruce: "Come home so we can flush together." Only rural folks with a holding tank can understand the pure joy we felt knowing that a septic pumper truck had maneuvered down and back up our icy driveway, taking away 3,500 gallons of waste water. "Amen," I texted back, the experience simultaneously romantic and religious. Chippewa Septic owner Travis Simet is my hero.

"Everything's a little harder in the country," a friend told Bruce and me when we first moved to our Lake Hallie cabin. Six months in, our septic system failed. Given his extensive research, Bruce still claims he could earn a degree in septic management (or should I say Private Onsite Wastewater Treatment Systems—POWTS). Modern zoning meant we'd have to install two concrete holding tanks, nose to nose and specially cast to fit the long configuration of our lot. This was summer. Of course, we didn't consider we'd likely have to call a septic pumper twice per winter. Or that a truck would have to maneuver our steep, quarter-mile driveway, which becomes a little like the Donner Pass from December through February. Or that I'd have to spread a thousand pounds of salt and sand, sifting the mixture off the back of my plastic snow sled, a low-tech but efficient approach, just so the truck could get to us.

Our "pump guy" before Travis was easygoing and chatty. "What are you gonna do about it?" he'd say about the state of politics or pretty much anything else. Then, his not-so-chatty son took over. We'd see him every two months, and we built a relationship. In early January, I called for a pump. "The driveway is perfectly clear," I pitched, knowing Son was warier than Dad. An hour later, a receptionist called back: "We thank you for your business, but we can't come to your house in the winter."

Our tanks hold four thousand gallons of waste; an alarm rings when we get to three thousand. I did the math: we had room for about three more weeks of flushing, showering, and laundering. No need to panic.

I got off the phone and panicked. I texted friends with septic systems, then I went old school and checked the yellow pages. In desperation, I called all three numbers listed for Chippewa Septic. A few minutes later, Travis called me. I explained the driveway and the current conditions.

"I've got a few dicey ones," Travis said confidently. "Can I come today?"

I talked with him while he moved away the cement tank cover and dropped the large hose in. Afterward, he came to the door, rubber boots on my outside mat, body leaning toward me. Even though his boots were clean and my house has a "no need to take your shoes off" policy, this must have been septic guy protocol, like putting on the big rubber gloves when he touched anything outside the truck and taking them off before he wrote the invoice. Surprisingly, the discovery that bacteria in human waste can cause illness didn't occur until the 1850s. One hundred and seventy years later, Travis offered me a bill with clean hands.

I told him, "Our alarm goes off about every two months. I'll see you in the spring."

Bruce and I will never again be one of those "flush and forget" people. And neither will any of our guests. Above our toilet, my framed homemade sign reads: "If it's yellow, let it mellow...." You know the rest. Bottom line: every flush counts.

Chippewa Septic was established in 1966 and has been a father/ son business ever since. Travis Simet and his wife, Cassi, took over from Travis's dad, Steve Simet, in 2018. Steve had worked as an over-the-road truck driver for twenty-four years and wanted an occupation that meant he could be home each night. Through a friend, he heard Chippewa Septic was for sale. Steve went on a few runs with the owner and bought him out in 2000. Steve moved the business from Lake Wissota to south of Eau Claire where he lived. Travis started going on jobs with his dad when he was a kid. The current shop is just a few miles down the road from Steve's, next to Travis and Cassi's house. Their motto: "It's Important to Have It Done Properly."

About 30 percent of Wisconsin homes have a septic system other than city water and sewer, and that number is even higher in Chippewa County, where over 50 percent of total housing units have POWTS. In contrast, only 22 percent of housing units in Eau Claire County have them. Human waste management is a solid business in the Chippewa Valley. Cassi reports that Travis often goes weeks without a day off. Perhaps only owning a funeral home or liquor store would offer as much security in this area. As one septic website proclaims: "The more it flows, the better we eat."

I ask the Simets if Travis had to deal with any bathroom humor when classmates discovered what his dad did for a living. Steve and Travis laugh and recall how Steve sometimes dropped his son off at middle school in the septic truck. Travis says, "And he blew the air horn."

Both father and son lament the downsides of the job: smashed fingers from heavy cement tank covers, mosquitoes, poison ivy, bees, rain, heat, and bitter cold. These are unexpected answers, given I really want to know about the dirty business of handling strangers' waste. Travis says simply that this line of work "takes a certain kind of person." His dad nods in agreement.

Many septic businesses are passed down through families, most often father to son. Travis explains this is partly because sixteen hundred hours of work experience are required for a Septage Servicing Operator certification, which means it's often easiest for a parent to hand the business off to a child who's already logged hours of experience. I ask Travis about any siblings who might want to work in the business with him. "My sister is a nurse," he tells me. "I couldn't do her job any more than she could do mine."

Bruce and I are glad he does this job. We know the relief of an empty septic tank: if you can flush, all is right in your world.

The Eagle Man of Eau Claire

I stood outside of Lake Hallie Golf's clubhouse with my clamshell of leftover fried walleye when an older gentleman showed me a sixteen- by twenty-inch photo in a plastic sleeve. The two eagles on the print seemed nearly life size.

"Do you want to buy this?" he pitched.

We'd never seen each other before. Don Larson had no idea I was writing a column about eagles on Lake Hallie; I didn't know I'd just stumbled upon the Eagle Man of Eau Claire—a title his friend once silkscreened onto a T-shirt for him.

Don regularly photographs five eagles' nests around the Chippewa Valley, including one across the road from Lake Hallie Golf's fourth hole, where that particular photo was snapped. Don recently compiled a fifty-eight-page book, *I Am the Eagle: Compelling Facts and Photos of Bald Eagles*, which he sells out of his car.

Eagles are a part of my daily life on Lake Hallie. They nest along our shore, and I hear their distinct screech throughout the day. Even after living here for years, my city-slicker husband, Bruce, still gets excited watching eagles pluck fat sunfish from the lake or hover over a family of swimming otters.

I was recently kayaking at dusk when I noticed a large female roosting in my neighbor's tallest tree. Looking up thirty feet, I was struck by her straight-backed magnificence, her gold beak and talons against the lush green foliage. That night, her cry was louder and more urgent than usual. A smaller male flew past her and brushed the full front of her with the tips of his wings. One swoop. He soared high then fell into a steep dive toward the female. Two swoops. I could hear the whoosh of the male's five-foot wingspan as he approached his mate. Three swoops. Four.

The female flew toward the male. Over my head, the two locked talons and did a freefall. I paddled fiercely, determined not be hit by amorous fowl, no matter how great a story it would make.

Later, I discovered this midair tussle is called a cartwheel courtship flight. Afterward, they mated in a nearby tree. I looked up Walt Whitman's "The Dalliance of Eagles," a poem Mr. Crowe taught us in tenth grade: "A living, fierce, gyrating wheel, / Four beating wings, two beaks, a swirling mass tight grappling." Back then, did I giggle when I learned what the word *dalliance* meant? I'm sure I did. Now, I know the astounding experience of witnessing such a dalliance.

Given Americans' 50 percent divorce rate, we may find it romantic that eagles pair up for life. The year-round open water and access to fish on parts of Lake Hallie mean that dallying couple may have lived here as long as Bruce and I have.

Even three decades ago, this pair would have been a rare sight on Lake Hallie or anywhere in the country. Acid rain killed fish (eagles' main source of sustenance), pesticides like DDT caused reproduction issues, and mercury and lead poisoned them. Despite the bird's status as a symbol of American strength and freedom—one emblazoned on most of our currency—the eagle population was nearly decimated.

Since 1940, the Bald Eagle Protection Act has prohibited people from harming or disturbing eagles, but it was the Endangered Species Act of 1973 that banned chemicals and habitat disruption and that eventually contributed to a resurgence of eagles. The American bald eagle—which is not actually hairless: the name comes from the old English word *balde*, meaning white—was one of the first species listed as endangered. In 2007, it was reclassified from endangered ("close to extinction") to threatened ("at risk of being endangered").

❧

Weeks after meeting Don Larson, I join him for a drink at Lake Hallie Golf. He says the only eagles he saw as a kid were in a zoo. He grew up in Eau Claire and graduated from Memorial High School in 1959, the spring after Buddy Holly died. He was a fan long before Holly's plane crash, and he later became a Holly expert and music historian. His photos from Holly's last concert at the legendary Eau Claire venue Fournier's Ballroom in January 1959 appear in John Goldrosen's biography of the singer and in Waylon Jennings's autobiography. Don wrote a memoir in 2018, titled *To Me They Weren't Stars, They Were Just My Friends*, which recounts his time with Holly and Jennings, as well as John Denver.

During the spring and summer, Don sits across the road from the fourth hole for up to five hours a day, camera on his lap, watching a nest in a tall pine for the eagle pair he's dubbed Ozzie and Harriet. One of Don's photos of them hangs at Lake Hallie Golf. He says, "I've never seen a bald eagle I didn't like. It's just a thrill to be close to them."

As we chat at the clubhouse, golfers come to our table and ask about his eagles. He finds other eagle lovers, he tells me, like "two fishermen who ask each other 'how they biting?' " He often sells them his prints.

❧

If Don is the Eagle Man of Eau Claire, then the Wisconsin Department of Natural Resources (DNR) research scientist and eagle expert Laura Jaskiewicz is the Eagle Woman of Wisconsin, though no one has yet made her a T-shirt. She and other DNR biologists travel the state observing nests and monitoring the growing eagle population. She tells me, "I have always loved birds and wildlife. This led me to devote my life to protecting animals and their natural habitats." If anyone discovers an eagle's nest anywhere in Wisconsin, Laura wants to know.

In 1983, the Northern States Bald Eagle Recovery Plan emerged as a recommendation from one of five regional teams created under authority of the Endangered Species Act (ESA) to propose specific strategies for saving threatened species. Their team members—fish and wildlife, land management, and park service officers along with a zoology professor—wrote, "The Plan is based on biological considerations and does not attempt to resolve social and political issues."

Since January 2017, the ESA has been under attack—and threats have recently become more dire. Newly proposed provisions to the law could mean the federal government will consider the economic impact of saving a species rather than making a decision based solely on science. If these provisions pass, oil and gas companies and the logging industry would not be restricted from drilling or cutting in areas where endangered species live. In addition, manufacturers would no longer have to deal with the "regulatory burden" of pollution laws.

If the ESA goes extinct, likely so will 1,663 species of protected plants and animals. Right now, 1,275 are endangered and 388 are threatened—numbers that increase each year. The eagles on Lake Hallie are a concrete example of the tremendous impact the ESA has made over these past forty-six years and one of many reasons the law must continue to exist without provisions.

Don Larson sets up his eagle-viewing camera for his own enjoyment but also, he says, "to get kids away from videogames." He loves it when neighbors with young children join him on his lookouts. His mission is to ensure that our great-grandchildren will enjoy watching eagles in the wild and not just view them in old photos, like drawings of the long-gone dodo bird (last seen in 1681) or passenger pigeon (gone since 1914). About his Eagle Man moniker, Don says, "I would gladly share the title with anybody."

Date Cutters

You might not expect retired stone engraver Billy Krause's story to read like the adventures of a wayfaring musician, but that's exactly what he is. He bought his first guitar in the summer of 1962—as he headed into seventh grade—with fifteen dollars in lawn-mowing earnings. Around age sixteen, he performed one Friday night a month with his Regis High friends in their group, 8 Penny Opera, at Fournier's Ballroom, the pinnacle of venues long before there was an Eau Claire music scene. Louis Armstrong, Glen Miller, Tommy Dorsey, Buddy Holly, Bobby Darin, and other legends ghosted that same stage on nights when Billy played. On weekends, he watched bands through the front window of the Wagon Wheel on Wisconsin Street or through the backdoor of the Diamond Lounge (now the Fire House). After high school, Billy hitchhiked along the East Coast with only a guitar and a duffle. He played for tips on the street, partied with other hippies, and sometimes slept in Goodwill collection bins filled with soft clothes.

Billy returned home to Eau Claire in 1971, the same year Fournier's closed, and landed a job at Johnson Monument, LLC. He studied under owners Don and Keith Johnson. Billy still calls Don "an incredible graniteer who knew the old school techniques." Billy learned the trade—manual work with the finesse of an artist—and spent the next four decades working stone with a sandblaster and chisel. He retired in 2016 from Lifetime Memorials, a subsidiary of Johnson, though Billy says, "Death was my employer."

Seven years ago, my nephew Mitch See answered an ad in the *Leader-Telegram* and went to work for Billy. For each man, a life unfolded as a "final date engraver," someone who cuts into stone people's last day on earth. Their handiwork may be seen in these same area cemeteries hundreds of years from now.

A recent PBS documentary, *Into the Night: Portraits of Life and Death*, explores the great mystery of death: some believe it's a portal to the afterlife, others see it as a final stop in this life. As a young man, Billy considered cutting names and dates as just a job. Then, he says, "I cut the first stone of a person I knew, and that changed everything. And the first time I cut an infant marker after I had children of my own, I never saw a marker for a young person the same again."

He met his wife in 1976 at Adler's, the bar he managed then. He remembers Margie wearing a brown corduroy jumpsuit. Just after spotting her, Billy told his buddy he was going to marry that woman. At the time, Billy and Margie were both seeing other people. On their first date, he stood her up; but she didn't care because she had a back-up man that night. Now, he calls her Spark, short for sparkplug, and he is her Billy Boy. They've been together for forty-three years.

A year ago at our place, Billy pointed at a house across the lake. I told him, "Helen Sabaska lives there."

"Related to Clark Hughes?" he asked.

"His daughter. How did you know Clark?"

"I cut his wife's date," he said. "We got to be friends." This happens to Billy often. After frequenting bars and cemeteries for most of his life, he seems to know everyone. I told him Helen's husband had just died. Like many people, Helen and Jerry invested in their stones long before they needed them—the names and birthdays were there just waiting for the final dates. But the first time Helen visited their graves, Jerry's death date was carved onto her headstone.

"Someone wasn't looking at his paperwork," Billy chuckled.

During Billy's first year of retirement, he recorded his fourth solo album, which he deemed his final one, appropriately named *Last Call*. His songs are like his stories: easy to listen to and woven through with observations of everyday life. One interviewer called him the Woody Guthrie of western Wisconsin. In "Ballad of Farewell," he croons, "When I'm gone I'll be resting in a cool dry place." He sings a line from a Holly Williams tune, "Why you drinkin' like the night is young?"—something he might have overheard from a corner table at the Diamond Lounge.

Earlier this summer, my husband and I gathered with a small crowd on the patio of Lake Hallie Golf to hear Billy's trio, The Porter Brothers, play music on a late Sunday afternoon. Between songs, he asked, "What do you get when you cross lefse and LSD?" Billy deadpanned, "A trip to Eleva." Everyone here knows that village, home to many Norwegians.

The crowd laughed. Before the set was over, Margie started to feel a little strange. She experienced a tingling sensation down one arm. A nurse friend in the audience did a quick assessment. Margie was having stroke. Billy cut it short and rushed his Spark to the hospital in seven minutes, half the usual drive time.

Two weeks later, they come over for a pontoon ride on Lake Hallie with Bruce and me. My nephew Mitch and his wife, Abby, join us, the first time the six of us have been together since Mitch and Abby's 2017 wedding when Billy played at their reception.

I ask Margie how she's doing. "Oh, I'm fine," she says over a glass of wine. "I just gotta take a baby aspirin."

Billy has been managing his blood cancer for a while, but Margie's sudden stroke rattled them both. In his song "Ghost," he laments: "Wait up by the bend, I'll be coming right behind you."

Billy tells me, "No matter who goes first, we're gonna have one hell of a party." Ironically, the master headstone carver and his wife will be cremated; they do not plan to have their own markers made. "We're not cemetery visitors," Margie says.

I pontoon the six of us down Lake Hallie to see Clark Hughes's old farmstead, playing tour guide on this lake I adore. Mitch, Billy, and Bruce sit in front; Abby, Margie, and I gather in back, segregated by gender, as happens at most family parties I throw. I can't hear the men, but I watch Mitch rub the back of his hand across his beard, the way he does when he's thinking.

Like Billy, Mitch respects the work and his old mentor. I gave Mitch a pocket notebook to write what he sees on the job and record the kind of stories Billy used to relay: about being alone in a cemetery, cutting the final date of a person's life in stone, how humbling it is to be what Billy calls "the last audience to that last act of that life."

Months after Billy retired, Bruce and I took Mitch and Abby to dinner following a literary event. Old friends joined us at the table. "How do you all know each other?" someone asked.

"I changed this one's diapers," I said, pointing at thirty-something Mitch. "Now he's the new Billy Krause."

"No," Mitch protested. "I can't sing. I just cut dates."

The Bird Man of Chippewa Falls

Generations of Chippewa Falls children knew family doctor Charles Kemper as "the Bird Man." Southside kids like me often rode our bikes through the alley behind his Maple Street house just to get a glimpse of the caged raptors he fostered, including a turkey vulture named Maurice.

Doc Kemper turned one hundred years old in December 2019. He'd been an MD for so long, the babies he delivered grew up to have babies—and he delivered those, too. He once called medicine his "vocation" and the study of birds his "avocation." He hung up his stethoscope in the early 1990s, but he'll be a bird lover forever.

As a licensed volunteer for the US Fish and Wildlife Service for many years, Dr. Kemper captured birds and attached tiny aluminum or stainless-steel numbered ankle bracelets around even tinier legs. The image that comes to my mind is a monitor for house arrest, though banding birds is quite different from confining felons to their homes. The birds are encouraged to fly away so humans can trace their routes. Once banded and released, birds are caught elsewhere so their movement, sometimes spanning continents, can be reconstructed. On his ninety-second birthday eight years ago, Dr. Kemper celebrated the 92,000 birds he had banded. All data—which offers clues on migration, behavior, reproduction, lifespan, and survival—is sent to the central US Geological Survey's Bird Banding Laboratory.

Doctoring and birding were intertwined for Dr. Kemper almost from the beginning. His interest in feathered friends was sparked out of boredom as an Army Air Corps flight surgeon whose first trip across the Pacific took thirty days, often skirting typhoons that churned up three-story waves. He passed mundane hours aboard ship by watching the majestic albatross and other seabirds. He still recalls how the fulmars and shearwaters flew "straight as an arrow" a few feet above the sea, shearing waves with their wings.

"When you're all alone," Dr. Kemper wrote fifteen years after World War II, "just a speck floating on the great ocean, you soon find a kinship to other living things that keep you company."

Kemper grew up in Baltimore. After medical school, he was drafted and sent to military training in Texas, where he met Wisconsin native Margaret Johnson. They married in July 1945, just three weeks before he shipped out. Though the war ended while he was at sea, Kemper continued on to Okinawa. After his military service and further training at Harvard, he and Margaret settled in Chippewa Falls, and Dr. Kemper began his career as a general practitioner.

"We did everything," he told the *Wall Street Journal* in 2018. "We delivered babies and did appendectomies and gall bladders." He considered himself a country doctor. For over forty years, he made house calls, something almost unimaginable today given modern HMOs and medical centers so big they have separate campuses. I remember pedaling to his home office in 1982 for a sports physical with the three dollar payment in my sock. Today, that visit may cost a hundred times more.

One of Kemper's former patients, Brad Sweitzer, told me, "Dr. Kemper helped my mother bring me into this world, and he was my doctor for many years." As a kid, Brad sliced his tongue on a door hinge, and Doc stitched him up. Apparently, this freak accident was worthy of documentation. When teenaged Brad went for an appointment, Dr. Kemper showed him the photograph of his injured tongue. I would guess Brad never ran in the house with his tongue out again.

Back then, making house calls and getting to know patients from birth through adulthood were part of a small-town doctor's role. Even today, wherever he goes, people still thank Doc Kemper.

His compassion extended beyond human patients. Not long after he moved here, he founded the Chippewa Wildlife Society to promote sanctuary and refuge to animals. Word spread.

A farmer once showed up in Dr. Kemper's office cradling a colt with a broken leg. A veterinarian suggested putting it down, but Doc set the colt's leg with four *Reader's Digest* magazines and a plaster cast. Even local game wardens brought wounded creatures his way. St. Joseph's Hospital allowed him to x-ray birds. Year after year, his backyard was full of on-the-mend fowl and other critters. Once, while one of his human patients was in labor, Dr. Kemper carried an injured chipmunk in his lab coat pocket. He swears that mother named her baby Chip.

After a roadrunner hitched a ride in an open U-Haul with a couple moving from California to the Chippewa Valley in 1990, Dr. Kemper nursed the dehydrated and starving "ground cuckoo" by feeding it minnows. Kids from all over town came to see this bird—exotic for Wisconsin—and to ask why it didn't say "beep-beep" like in the cartoons. Roadrunners don't migrate, so this stray rode back home to Twentynine Palms on a Delta flight; a park ranger released it into the wild.

Starting in 1957, either Dr. Kemper or one of his fellow volunteers visited a local TV tower every day during spring and fall migrations to count birds that had collided with the thick guy-wires holding up the communication towers. On the worst night, he tells me, birds fell from the sky like rain. I get a lump in my throat when just one of my beloved black-capped chickadees or American finches flies into our picture window. Who can imagine the horror of counting more than ten thousand dead bodies by hand?

"I guess if I wasn't such a nut, I wouldn't have bothered with it," he told Duke University's alumni publication *Duke Magazine*.

One might call him obsessed. I do the math: migration seasons last at least thirty straight days, so that adds up to sixty days a year for forty-five years. That means Dr. Kemper spent approximately seven years of his life waking up before dawn to count avian deaths. In 1996, he published a paper about his findings in *The Passenger Pigeon*, the Wisconsin Society for Ornithology's journal. Even coming from a "citizen scientist," Dr. Kemper's decades-long study was well respected by bird specialists around the country, including Chandler Robbins, senior author of *Birds of North America* in the Golden Field Guides series, who acknowledged Kemper's work as a major contribution.

Dr. Kemper counted live birds, too. He organized the first Christmas Bird Count in Chippewa County and participated in it for fifty-eight years, almost half of the 120 years that the Audubon Society had been sponsoring the nationwide event. Dr. Kemper's 2007 book, *Birds of Chippewa Land: Long-term Study of Bird Populations in Chippewa, Eau Claire, and Neighboring Counties*, further documented his work. The centenarian tells me, "There is a story for each species."

To call him a birder is like saying Fred Astaire was a fine dancer or Kobe Bryant was a pretty good ballplayer.

There is no telling the number of lives Doc Kemper has helped save: from young soldiers to Chippewa county residents—human and animal—to billions of birds flying through Wisconsin, cared for and counted by the Bird Man of Chippewa Falls.

Our Miss Victory

As an eighteen-year-old, Winifred "Winnie" Rubenzer didn't run a rivet gun like Rosie the Riveter. Instead, she and her coworkers at the Eau Claire Ordnance Plant—many of them sisters, wives, or sweethearts of US service members—served our country by making ammunition during World War II.

Winifred is now ninety-four, and she goes by the name Freddie Glass Jensen. Evidence of her patriotism is scattered around her Chippewa Falls home, built for her by her second husband. In a portrait of herself as "Miss Victory," featured in a poster to promote the war effort, she stands in her drab munitions-worker coveralls, rifle grenade raised over her head and 35 mm shell clasped in her arm. On another wall, I spot an award for her seventeen years of service to the Chippewa County Historical Society near a framed invitation to President Obama's inauguration. When I ask about her connection to the president, she says, "Oh honey, I donated *a lot* of money to him."

She eagerly shares her stories and her scrapbooks of photos, news articles, and letters. Freddie prepared for our meeting by calling her friend in Cleveland, ninety-five-year-old Irish, who worked with her at two munitions plants. Freddie offers me some significant dates. In August 1942, US Rubber was bought by the government and converted to an ammunition factory, Eau Claire Ordnance Plant (now Banbury Place). Freddie's father worked there as an electrician, commuting from their Tilden farm. In July 1943, young Winnie, a recent graduate of McDonell Memorial High School in Chippewa Falls, met a woman named Lillian in a long line to apply at the ordnance plant. The two of them were hired as "inspectresses" in the Bullet Visual department and became fast friends. Soon Lillian changed her name to Irish.

"Because she was from Ireland?" I ask.

"No," Freddie chuckles, "because she liked it." Her friend inspired her. Freddie always hated the name Winnie, and not long after she befriended Irish, she met her first husband, George Glass, an Air Force cadet at the Eau Claire State Teachers College. That night, Winifred decided not to change her name, but, as she says, to "just use the rear end of it." She's been Freddie ever since.

"The plant was open around the clock," she tells me. "I worked all hours." She and Irish rented a room on Main Street and walked to the plant on Wisconsin Street. They worked side by side, inspecting trays of bullets for dents eight hours a day or more, if needed.

When the ammunition plant ceased production in December 1943 and returned to producing rubber, the two women set off on their next adventure: a transfer to the Green River Ordnance Plant. In January, Freddie and Irish rode the bus to Dixon, Illinois, where for almost a year they slept in barracks and ate in a mess hall. "Just like soldiers," she says. At first, they admired the other women's "brilliantly red hair," but after using shared showers, they realized that the unnaturally red hair was not limited to the women's heads.

Soon Freddie and Irish noticed their own hair developing a red hue, they suspected from the chemicals. "We wondered what it did to our insides," Freddie says with a laugh. They worked in a large bay, filling rifle grenades with liquid pentolite. Freddie describes how she stood at the assembly line and pulled a rope to open a spout overhead, allowing hot pentolite—similar to TNT—to ooze into waiting rifle grenades. Conditions were sweltering. Freddie remembers when one woman blew herself up when she crammed a shell into the line too forcefully. According to the National Park Service, the factories were so dangerous that between the 1941 Pearl Harbor bombing and the 1944 D-Day invasion, the United States saw more industrial deaths than military casualties.

I tear up. "I can't even imagine what the world was like then," I tell Freddie.

She says, "I don't remember being unhappy." After all, she tells me later, "Illinois had many popular dance halls."

Freddie and Irish worked at the plant until they married their sweethearts just as the war ended. Second Lieutenant George Glass earned his wings, then he and Freddie lived in Pennsylvania, George's home state, before moving back to the Chippewa Valley in 1946. George died in 1989.

"Between husbands," Freddie tells me, she traveled the world on her own: China, Russia, and Europe. She married Wayne Jensen when they were both seventy-two, and they enjoyed seven years together before his death.

Freddie is still an artist and sometimes-writer, a gardener and genealogist. For the past thirty years, she's done triweekly water exercise at the YMCA, her key to good health. Her driver's license is valid until her one hundredth birthday.

I gush over the stunning teenaged Freddie posing as Miss Victory. Her photo appeared on posters around town and in newspapers throughout Illinois: "Bring those sons and sweethearts home. . . . Get out the ammunition at Green River Ordnance Plant."

"Josie got a lot more copy than I did," Freddie says.

"Rosie," I correct.

First came the song "Rosie the Riveter," released in January 1943: "She's making history / working for victory." Five months

Freddie Rubenzer posing as Miss Victory for Green River
Ordnance Plant in 1944. COURTESY OF FREDDIE GLASS JENSEN

later, Norman Rockwell's cover of *The Saturday Evening Post* por-
trayed to more than three million subscribers his rendition of
a muscular bomber-factory worker with red painted nails and
ROSIE chalked on her black lunch pail, her loafer squashing a
copy of Hitler's *Mein Kampf.*

Rosie was propaganda; Freddie is reality. She worked in difficult circumstances to help win the war, married twice and raised
five children, thrived as an executive secretary at Northwestern
Bank, cared for her aging parents, volunteered in her community,
added to the beauty of the world with her flowers and paintings,

offered hugs when people needed them, and always looked forward to her next challenge.

Ironically, the most recognizable Rosie today was little known in 1943. The "We Can Do It" poster was an internal campaign at Westinghouse Electric featuring a worker with her hair pulled up in a red polka-dot kerchief, fist raised and bicep flexed. In the 1980s, this Rosie became an iconic image of the women's movement, particularly for working women and some unions. In 1999, she appeared on a US postage stamp.

Syndicated journalist Alice Hughes wrote on July 14, 1943: "Probably the most popular pet name around the country for a woman factory worker is Rosie the Riveter." Seventy-six years later, Freddie shows me a commendation from her supervisor on Eau Claire Ordnance Plant letterhead: "We have found her very efficient, courteous, and commandable." These were considered admirable qualities for a woman entering the workforce, but many of these Rosies, like Freddie, evolved into so much more throughout their long careers: leaders, trailblazers, and mentors.

Since 2017, National Rosie the Riveter Day—March 21— celebrates the sixteen million women who joined the workforce during World War II.

Today, any woman working outside of her home can thank those teen-through-middle-aged assembly line workers for leading the way. Each of them forever represents a small part of something big.

"Well," Freddie says now, "somebody had to do it."

Lake Hallie Spirits

I don't exactly see apparitions at my house on Lake Hallie, but sometimes I sense a presence. My husband doubts me, though Bruce knows that in each place we live we leave behind pieces of ourselves: children's growth etched onto a wall or dead skin lost between floorboards. Why wouldn't we also create a spiritual imprint?

Many of us pick up on the vibes in any space. When you walk into a room where two people are angry at each other or one in which a couple is newly in love, that energy is palpable. The same is true with psychic phenomena.

Paranormal investigator Dan Sturges claims that everyone has a bit of an "ability." He says, "It's like cable TV and basic service versus premium service. Everybody's got basic—you need basic. But some people have HBO. Some people have Showtime. Some people have all of it plus Internet and on demand."

My antenna has always been able to tune into that which I cannot see. I'm not alone. One night not long after Bruce and I moved to Lake Hallie, a friend visited. After maybe fifteen minutes sitting at the kitchen counter, she looked up from her Summer Shandy and said, "You have a ghost, don't you?" This felt a bit like someone with a cat allergy sniffing out a hidden kitten.

I nodded. "I think he likes to be right here," I said, pointing to

the hallway, "especially when we drink." I joked that we just live
and let live at our new place.

Our house's documents only go back to the 1960s, when the
first septic system was installed, but the most interesting history
comes from my old-timer neighbors. They claim that in the 1920s,
this was an early site for Lake Hallie Golf's clubhouse, then for a
small cabin built by Banty Wendt. Next, ownership shifted from
one Tangen family—Art and Rita, longtime owners of the golf
course—to another: Art's cousin George and his wife, Joan. We
bought it from Joan in 2010, ten years after George died in the
house.

When I started recording the oral histories of people who
have been on Lake Hallie the longest, my neighbors connected
me with Nellie Dutton Erickson, who lives across the lake from
us. I called to set up a meeting, and Nellie told me, "I met my
husband at your house, October 31st, 1946."

My initial reaction: Does she really know where I live? I soon
discovered that Nellie knows everything. She spent her entire life
here, and her ancestors were some of the original white settlers
in this area.

I first visit her just after Halloween in 2014. "Witches were in
our family," she teases. "Not just me."

After providing an hour's worth of Lake Hallie history—
including lore about its namesake, lumber baron John Ure's
daughter Hallie, who may have drowned here—Nellie proclaims,
"Now I'm going to tell you the story of your house."

Nellie lived off of a busy highway, what's now OO. Her dad,
Gilbert Dutton, owned Bucket of Blood Bar, next door to Slim's.
Gilbert died in 1933, when Nellie was a baby. As a girl, she ran
with a group of neighborhood kids. Over seventy years later, she
remembers there were three girls and fourteen boys. She still calls
them "Hallie Brats." Each Halloween, they snuck onto Banty's

yard—which now belongs to Bruce and me—and tipped over the outhouse. Once, they pushed so hard, it ended up in the lake.

I know where that outhouse stood. One winter a few years ago, a sinkhole opened up in our side yard, precisely where the long-ago owners kept their latrine.

It may be easy to cast Frank "Banty" Wendt as the neighborhood ogre, but perhaps he just didn't like kids tipping over his outhouse. He was born in Germany in 1893 and settled in Eau Claire with his parents and siblings. Later he built two small cabins on Lake Hallie, where he rented boats and sold bait. Nellie tells me Banty also worked as a handyman at the golf course. His obituary in 1971 listed him as a bricklayer. He erected both of his rustic structures on stone—one perched on a shale outcropping on the south edge of Lake Hallie and the other, which is where I'm writing from, built into rock with its foundation in the water.

One of my other neighbors claims Banty got his nickname because he strutted around like a bantam rooster. Others confirm he was small and aggressive—a hothead with a mean streak, especially when he drank. He often picked fights with the biggest guys in Slim's. No surprise: Banty got beat up time and again.

On Halloween when Nellie was fourteen, her neighborhood pack snuck onto Lake Hallie Golf Course, down Banty's long driveway, and toward the outhouse. But before they could push it over, Banty jumped out from behind the narrow door with a shotgun and sprayed rock salt in their direction. The petrified kids scattered.

Nellie stumbled as she tried to run away. Her friend David, a seventh grader who was already six-foot-two and had "legs like Ichabod Crane," jumped over the top of her and kept running. She fell again trying to get up the steep, sandy driveway. But as she struggled to climb over the barbed-wire fence, a pair of hands reached down, lifting her up and over to safety. This was the first time Nellie met Jim Erickson, a nineteen-year-old who had just moved to the area so he could keep his prized horse, Colonel, on his sister's farm.

After that Halloween encounter, Jim waved at Nellie as she waited for the bus. Nellie says she didn't really notice him. Then their mothers talked at a church function, and Mrs. Erickson told Mrs. Dutton that Jim was smitten with Nellie.

When Nellie's mom asked about this boy, Nellie responded, "Jim who?" But once Nellie turned sixteen, the two started dating. That neighborhood prank changed the course of Nellie's life. She and Jim married in 1954. Nellie is now eighty-eight; her beloved Jim died in 2010. She still calls him her "perfect man."

Not many ghost stories turn out to be love stories. Nellie didn't help me identify my house ghost, but she did renew my belief that we're all just passing through, one chance encounter after another.

How We Spend Our Days

The See family, circa 1934, including the author's father (in overalls with his mother's hand on his shoulder). COURTESY OF PATTI SEE

Family Delicacy

One night when I visit Dad, he's got Mom's cookbooks laid out on the table.

"What are you looking for?" I ask. He became quite the cook after my mom got sick and he had to take over her jobs in their home: cooking, cleaning, laundry. He experimented with chili until he perfected his recipe. He even made popovers a few times. And he often looked for new recipes to try. In many ways, he took his fix-it-guy knack for making something new out of re-purposed parts in his garage and adapted it to the kitchen. Some of his dishes—bologna with noodles comes to mind—were the culinary equivalent of his once making a cribbage board out of a toilet seat.

"Well, I tell you what," he says. "Someone brought me a whole squirrel and I gotta figure out how to cook it." He's got the cleaned squirrel carcass in a Ziploc bag on his kitchen counter.

As a girl, I often tagged along when my dad and brothers went squirrel hunting. I always believed that eventually one of them would let me shoot a gun. It never happened. My job was carrying the dead squirrels, which had usually been dropped inside a Wonder Bread bag. I still recall walking through the woods on cold November afternoons with warm dead squirrels brushing against my thigh. Once the squirrels were cleaned, I'm sure I played with the tails—some still with a bloody nub of tailbone attached. At least one of my brothers drove around town with a squirrel tail on his car antenna. We weren't really rednecks, though I realize these squirrely memories of mine don't support that claim. My only explanation is that this was the 1970s in small-town Wisconsin.

Each winter, Mom and Dad had a squirrel feed for neighbors and friends. I've never figured out if squirrels are difficult to clean or if they were just cleaned sloppily by my dad and brothers. In any case, as all of us ate tiny squirrel legs or the larger rib meat, we'd pull brown or gray squirrel hair out of our mouths. My mom often put a few "hair plates" on the table, so after we tugged squirrel hair from our teeth, we could deposit it on a separate plate. Was it too gross to put squirrel hair on your own dinner plate? It falls into the category of Stuff I Did in Childhood and Never Questioned Why, like getting clean in the same bathwater other siblings had just used or arguing with family members over who would get to eat the chicken butt—the fattiest part that went over the fence last. It sounded better than it was.

I look at this squirrel on my dad's counter and see that perhaps it is impossible to get all of the hair off of a skinned squirrel. The squirrel lies in a plastic bag, headless and pawless, like a backwoods mob victim.

I tell Dad, "I'd Google a recipe for squirrel." He looks at me blankly. "You know, look it up on the Internet."

Dad says, "What the hell does the Internet know about cooking squirrel?"

I remember how Mom used to dust the cut-up pieces in flour and brown them in her enormous cast iron skillet, then transfer the partially braised squirrel to an electric roasting pan for a few hours till the meat fell off the bone. I remember how tender and tasty it was, soaking in gravy, if you could just ignore the hair.

Dad's right: the Internet won't help him with what he's missing.

Fish Fry at Irvine

Tonight, we're a party of five: Dad and daughters and our husbands. Dad's been eager to try the fish fry at Irvine, the bar where he ate every weekday lunch for his nearly forty-year career on the Soo Line Railroad. When Dad first moved to Chippewa Falls in 1947, he rented a room above the bar and shared a grimy down-the-hall bathroom with other brakemen and engineers. They all lived just a hundred feet from the front door of the Soo yard office, where they punched their timecards.

The place has changed hands and names many times in the three decades since Dad retired. In just the last few years, it's been the Ghost Pub, the Depot, and now Pit Stop. Dad still calls it Irvine.

William Irvine ran the Chippewa Lumber & Boom Company in the mid-1880s, when it was the world's largest sawmill under one roof. He earned his riches in the logging business and donated 163 acres to Chippewa Falls in 1906. One hundred and thirteen years later, only that park and a street bear Irvine's name, though this ghost pub may still hold his spirit.

In 1870, when the railroad finally chugged into Chippewa Falls, this was one of the first hotels in town, catering to lumberjacks and other roughnecks. The rooms above the bar were let to prostitutes. That means in the same tiny rental where my dad wrote love letters to the girl who'd later become his wife, another girl spent time with smelly lumberjacks to make money for her family some seventy years earlier. Now, it's the ghost of himself my father might meet at this old tavern.

Tonight, I hold the door for Dad, and he uses his cane to hobble up the three concrete steps. Once inside, he walks from corner to corner, inspecting everything.

"Sure looks different in here," he says to our waitress. When Dad introduces himself—he always tells the server his name—she says she went to high school with my older brother, the other Joe See. I am reminded again how we are all connected in Chippewa Falls, like an intricate tapestry. Pull one thread and your neighbor's cousin frays a bit.

Dad walks up to the only other occupied table and says to the couple, "Well, you look familiar." At ninety, he can do this. Or maybe he always acted this way.

Turns out, they are his old neighbors, who moved off the Southside some forty years ago. They remain parishioners at Holy Ghost Church, like my dad. They tell Dad everything but their names.

I recognize the shape of the woman's face, but I can't pinpoint exactly how I know her. While I drink my Leinenkugel's and steal fries from Dad's plate, my brain sifts through my "face files" as I try to recall her name. At forty-eight, this happens to me frequently. It troubled me until I read an article that differentiated normal memory retrieval issues from full-blown dementia—my fear since my mom was diagnosed with Alzheimer's.

I smile in the direction of the couple. They are older than my sixty-nine-year-old husband, Bruce, but younger than Dad—in that no man's land where folks are happy to be alive and out for Friday night fish but not yet worried about moving into a nursing home.

After they finish their meal, the couple comes over to our booth. This older woman puts her face near mine. "Were you that little blondie who cried so hard when her mom dropped her off at kindergarten?"

Something clicks when I hear her voice. "Yes, I was," I say. Everyone in our booth laughs, and she does, too. I tell her, "I went to kindergarten through twelfth grade with your son." I search for his name.

She hugs me awkwardly from behind. "You're still as cute as ever." She rubs my dad's shoulder. "You have a beautiful family."

Dad nods and takes another bite of his beer-battered cod.

After the couple walks away from us, my sister Geralynn says, "You cried that hard in kindergarten?" What she means is: so hard that forty-three years later a woman in a bar remembers you for it?

"Yes. It was traumatic leaving Mom." Bruce smiles kindly in my direction. Geralynn shakes her head. She works as a kindergarten teacher's aide; she's seen it all. Dad keeps eating.

I look at Geralynn. "Remember that red polyester shirt Mom had? One with the white V-neck ribbing?" I tear up.

I know she remembers how just a few years ago we used to give Mom a bath every Saturday morning and how Mom worked the washcloth between her toes, like she did when she was a farm girl. When we lifted her out of the tub and toweled her off, Geralynn singing "Carwash" each time, Mom would giggle. We helped her get clean, and it meant the world: a steamy bathroom with the comforting scents of aloe shampoo and Pepsodent.

Mom would say to the two of us, "Oh, you girls," so full of affection, though she had no idea who we were. On those bath mornings, Mom was naked and vulnerable and all ours. We felt the same pressure of bringing a newborn home, only Mom was eighty-something and we were desperate and afraid in ways we never knew daughters could be.

Now, Geralynn nods in my direction.

I say, "Mom's red shirt had a tie at the top, like shoestrings. The first day of kindergarten I wrapped my fingers around the laces and wouldn't let go. Miss Dutton had to pry my hands off." This image is baked into my memory.

"How long did you cry?" she asks.

"Until November."

Again everyone at the table laughs, Dad until he coughs and coughs. His emphysema makes his laughter sound like gasps lassoed together.

Bruce toes my shoe under the table, a gesture that says, "You're quirky, and you're mine."

I say to Dad, "That woman? Her name was Sally Lea before she married."

"Yeah, that's right," Dad says. "Her parents owned a bakery in town. Sally Ann's Bakery. I think her ma and pa named it after their little girl." His eyes puddle.

Dad clears his throat and tells us, "Sally's sister married our mailman." It's just what Mom would have pointed out.

His Shirt Was Always Tucked In

My father and I share a disdain for long obituaries. We have other things in common: frizzy hair, the inability to drive past any good relics by the side of the road, a tendency to cry during *The Waltons*.

Both of us read obituaries daily—those in our thin *Chippewa Herald* and those in our thicker Eau Claire *Leader-Telegram*. He looks for people he knows; I look for stories.

A blatant lack of humility, before or after death, is one of my dad's triggers. He ridicules a stranger's four-column obit: "He did this, blah, blah, blah." As a writer, I know anything told in six hundred words would be better at three hundred. Or as a famous stand-up comedian learned from a particularly adept *New Yorker* editor: his humor pieces would be funnier if he left out some of the jokes. There is an art to omission. Dad dislikes long obituaries for the same reason he hates long sermons: *we get the picture.*

⁓

My father was forty-two when I was born. I'm the youngest of eight spanning nearly twenty years of babies. I didn't realize till I was past forty-two how much Dad and I are alike. We didn't really talk to each other until my mom got sick. Not that there was any unease; Dad simply let Mom do all of the talking. On the rare occasion when he actually answered the telephone, he'd talk for twenty seconds before saying, "Here's your mom."

After Alzheimer's hijacked Mom's mind and then her voice, Dad stepped up. Not only did he cook and clean for the two of them—quite the feat for a dude in his early eighties—he also seemed to take her place as family busybody. He started telling stories I'd never heard before, and he genuinely wanted to know the dull details of my life. He talked. A lot. He even gossiped once in a while.

At age eighty-nine, three years after my mom died, Dad seemed to succumb to the effects of a life well lived. In small-town Wisconsin, well-lived means he ate and drank and smoked as much as he liked as a younger man. Emphysema (now better known as COPD, or chronic obstructive pulmonary disease), diabetes, congestive heart failure, chronic anemia, and severe sleep apnea were slowing him down. No euphemisms—he was dying. One morning last summer, I awoke in a panic: I hadn't written his obituary.

We'd recently celebrated his eighty-ninth-and-a-half birthday at my house. I hung radio station bumper stickers (89.5!) from recessed lights and ceiling fans along with photos of him throughout his almost ninety years. We planned his party for months, but when the time came, he couldn't join us because he was in the hospital with pneumonia. Soon he'd go to a nursing home for rehab, then into a sleep study that determined he stopped breathing seventy times an hour, then home on oxygen full time with a CPAP machine that saved his life over and over again each night.

His color was gray. He tired easily. I believed this was the end, so I started writing.

Joe was born at home on the farm to Peter and Othilia (Schulhauser) See on January 18, 1926, the third of four children. During the Great Depression he lost his life's savings, $12.12, when the local bank collapsed. He moved to Chippewa Falls in 1947 for a job on the Soo Line Railroad, and he was a "Southsider" ever since. He worked his way up from switchman to yardmaster over 38 years and continued to love all things "Soo" even after he retired. Joe was a proud union member. He married Virgiline Weinfurter on September 1, 1948. They celebrated 64 years together before her death in 2012.

～

A year after I wrote those lines, he was still kickin' *and* living in his own home. He turned ninety that January—the milestone he looked forward to. Almost as soon as he'd blown out the candles at his birthday bash, he told me, "I think I can make it to ninety-one."

Then, in February, his appendix ruptured. Given his age and the condition of his heart and lungs, surgery was not an option. All of my siblings and some of our children came home to say goodbye. I finally finished the obituary I'd started months earlier. I was ready to let Dad go.

> For 90 years a farm boy from Junction City was a busy part of this world. He finally petered out on. . . .

Only a select few would know these are Joe See phrases—"I'm always busy," he'd say. Or about a small appliance that even *he* couldn't fix: "It just petered out."

Over many weeks, doctors flushed the sepsis from his body, and slowly he got better.

He's a tough old bird. There is no other explanation.

～

Recently, Dad's ninety-two-year-old neighbor died. As always, he and I discussed the obituary.

"Don't worry," I told Dad. "Yours isn't that long." He smiled. "It's just right. Not too long. Not too short."

"You wrote it already?" he asked.

"Finished it after your appendix burst. You want to see it?"

He shook his head.

A week later, we were sitting at his kitchen table again. "So anyway," he said. "What about my obituary?"

"You said you didn't want to see it."

"I didn't say *yes*, and I didn't say *no*." Classic Joe See coyness. At ninety-and-a-half, he can say and do whatever he likes, including change his mind.

He said, "Now the answer is *yes*."

"Okay," I said.

A few days later, he and I sit at his table on a Saturday morning. He's in his summer pin-striped robe; I'm in my cutoff jean shorts. Perhaps all my life our outfits have defined our roles in the family. He's the patriarch; I'm the baby, even as I near fifty years old.

I've printed and folded up the obit as if I'm going to mail it. I taped across the fold and wrote, "For your eyes only." I don't want him to share it with every visitor, the way he does with most emails, cards, invitations, and letters he receives.

He reads the outside of my folded paper, then he picks at the tape.

"Nope," I say. "Not until I leave." This is weird enough, I don't have to say.

"Hmmf," he grunts. He rubs his finger over the tape.

"I know you're curious, but I don't want to be here as you read it. And I don't want everyone to have a say in what to add or take out. Only you, okay?" "Dying by committee" was often what my mom's illness felt like. I don't want to deal with that again.

He nods, then sneaks a peek inside the paper without breaking the seal. He says, "Well, where's a picture of me? Don'tcha need a picture?" He chuckles.

I tell him he can choose. I suggest the church directory photo of him and my mom, the one we cropped *him* out of for her obituary. It's downright creepy when there's a stray family member's arm or spouse's ear in the departed's obit pic. In the photo I suggest, Mom and Dad are far enough apart that each can easily be cropped out.

We talk about whatever might have happened in the twenty hours since I last visited. How much rain's in his rain gauge? Who stopped by last night? Then we sit and read the paper together. I see him every day. Sometimes it's impossible to generate anything new to say, so we read or watch TV reruns.

As I back my car out of his driveway, I know he's breaking the seal on his obituary.

⌇

Dad will never know the difficulty I had in condensing ninety-plus years into three hundred words till only the most precise details remain.

> He gave blood religiously, and he voted in every election. His shirt was always tucked in.

That last line defines my father: not only his style of dress but also his attitude. He wouldn't be seen with his shirttails hanging out or even with his dress or work shirt sloppily hanging off his belt. How many of us kids were embarrassed time and again when Dad "discreetly" turned away from the conversation, dropped "trou" enough for just a bit of his tighty-whities to show—no matter who was there—and tucked in his shirt?

When my twenty-five-year-old son was a small boy, he once said to me, "You know what would be really funny? Grandpa Joe in a T-shirt." Had anyone *ever* seen Joe See in anything but a button down, usually plaid, shirt?

I realize that the details in his obituary are what Dad would never say about himself. He'd never confess: *He liked a bad joke and a good story.* But anyone who met Joe See will nod knowingly at this line.

⌇

Historically, the obituary (from the Latin *obit*, meaning death) was a legacy to honor aristocrats. Not until the late twentieth century did the common man obituary arise. Eventually, this led to celebrations of ordinary people with folksy tributes, thus the list of usually three items the deceased enjoyed. In our local paper, it's often the Green Bay Packers, something else, and grandchildren.

Obituary writing is an art, like any genre, but this suspension bridge between poetry and nonfiction has been reduced to asking loved ones to fill in the blank about the deceased. Another common practice is to prearrange funerals and obituaries. I can't help but think writing your own obituary is akin to giving yourself a nickname. What we may say about ourselves is likely not the legacy others will remember us by.

> Joe was a hands-on father when it was uncommon for dads to change diapers, wash clothes, or make "spit curls" in their daughters' hair. Still, he knew his place in the See house. He often told his kids, "Ask your mother." Joe was a hard worker who was always up to something: making cribbage boards out of toilet seats, re-webbing lawn chairs in his garage, or fiddling with flowers. He donated countless time and money to Holy Ghost parish, and he was part of a small, dedicated group that started the church picnic in 1975. He was active in the Knights of Columbus and cleaned more smelt than he cared to remember. Joe loved a bargain, and he was saving and reusing long before it was a trend. He could make something out of nothing, and he could fix just about anything. He started every Joe See tale with "So anyway . . ."

Death and grief expert Stephen Levine writes, "In the funeral home we put rouge on death. Even in the casket we deny our transiency." Sharing my dad's obituary with him was a way to wipe away death's rouge and acknowledge the extraordinary goodness in his long but quite ordinary life.

I ended his obit with a nontraditional suggestion, since we both agreed many years ago that very few mourners actually donate to the deceased's suggested recipient.

> Contributions on Joe's behalf can be made as follows: slip a few extra bucks in the church collection; donate blood, especially if you're a rare type like Joe; go to a thrift sale and pay the asking price; make something crafty, and give it away; have one more for the road.

Levine also says, "The only service one can do in a very real sense, whether in serving the dying or those who are healing themselves, is to remind people of their true nature—the uninjured, the deathless—which is the very source of healing." More than anything, I tried to portray my father's "true nature" in his obituary.

I figured he'd never mention it again. Then, a week after I dropped off his sealed obit, Dad says to me, "You know that church picnic I started?"

"Yeah." I know he won't offer a critique, but he will make corrections.

"It was in 1971, not 1975."

"Okay," I say. "Anything else you want me to change?"

"I can't think of a thing," he says. "Looks real good."

～

It's merely a coincidence that within a month of my sharing the obituary with Dad, his doctor tells him he no longer needs oxygen.

Dad thinks he's gotten away with something. He's not naïve

enough to believe he's cheated Mr. Death, but he does believe he's at least put him off a while longer. I realize Dad's still a sick man, but he seems brighter. More sparkle and less gray.

The respiratory company comes to pick up his compressor and spare tanks. No oxygen means he can ride with me the two hours to Uncle Robert's funeral. He and Dad married sisters, and they spent much of their early married lives together. Mom and Dad and their kids traveled each summer with Robert and Bernice's family. This was long before I was born, when each couple had seven kids and each cousin had a partner. When I consider four adults and fourteen young children, I think of crowd control and not a week's vacation. Back then, Dad was younger than I am now; because of our age difference, he always seemed old to me. Now he's one of the last surviving men in his family and my mom's, and somehow that makes me think of him as younger. He could easily pass for seventy-five. His mind is beyond sharp.

Recently we passed a farmer's field with six-foot-tall, hand-painted wooden roosters for sale. I slowed down so Dad could see them. "Wouldn't it be funny if I bought one for Bruce?" I asked. My husband loathes lawn ornaments, and my dad knows it. We both laughed and laughed.

"Get him two," Dad said. His eyes twinkled. "Tell him they are Bruce-sters."

Now that's the wordplay of a seventy-five-year-old.

Today, I offer to press Dad's trousers and help him pick out a shirt for Uncle Robert's funeral. While I'm in his basement laundry room waiting for the iron to heat up, I fold the ten pairs of underwear I washed on Saturday.

He still has a few pairs of tighty-whities left, though they are so washed-out they are more like loosey-dingies. Once I bleached a bucket of his white briefs so long they became a stew of cotton, and I had to sneak all of them into the garbage. I started doing his laundry last year after he came home from rehab and could no longer walk up and down the basement steps. After a week of dealing with graying whites, I suggested colored underwear.

"I wear white," he said.

"How about black?" I pitched. "No bleach needed." For his ninetieth birthday, I gave him a multipack that included bright blue. He never complained.

These details will not go in his obituary.

Today, when I carry up the laundry and his creased dress pants, I say, "If only Mom could see you in *blue* underwear."

"If only," Dad says.

Washtub

My father's voice sounds like Nick Nolte gargling marbles. Dad's almost ninety-one; I think of him as my baby. I feel the same flutter in my heart when I suspect something is wrong, the same crushing weight of responsibility and tenderness. At a glance, I can tell his mood, health, and disposition. Today, two steps into Dad's kitchen, I know he likely has pneumonia.

"It's a head cold, not a chest cold," he says. "I'm fine." For him, a common cold can turn deadly within hours: he could drown in his own juices if his lungs fill. His emphysema is from decades of breathing coal and diesel fumes, not to mention smoking for fifty years.

My sister and I rarely visit Dad at the same time, but this Saturday morning we're here together to decorate for Christmas. Geralynn and I tag-teamed our way through our mom's illness and death. Now we're doing the same for Dad.

He sends Geralynn and me to the garage rafters to find his toy train set, which he wants to pass on to a great-grandson. Geralynn climbs Dad's old wooden ladder, and I hold both sides. I stare at her calves while she looks through box after box, and we take turns talking each other into believing Dad really is a little better today.

After much poking around in layers of junk—some that's been

stacked neatly up here since before I was born—Geralynn finds the train box.

I spot an old washtub, the sort of farm relic that Pinterest-obsessed thirty-somethings search eBay for in order to accessorize a rented barn for an authentic "country wedding." Weeks ago, Dad said I could have it. "Take everything," he quipped. He stays in the house most of the time now. Each Sunday morning, as he shuffles to my car for a ride to church, he glances at the disorganized mess his garage has become and winces a little.

Geralynn carries the train inside, and I follow her with the Dura zinc alloy–coated Wheeling washtub. Dad sits at his kitchen table in his bathrobe, wheezing and reading the newspaper. His hair is slicked back, and wispy curls form around his enormous ears. Here's an irony: the bigger Dad's ears grow, the less he can hear.

I hold up the washtub. "It's got my name on it," I tease. I point at "P. See" written in marker across the side. Dad chuckles. We both know it was signed by my grandfather, Peter See, long before 1970 when he died of a heart attack. I was two; Dad was around my age now. Sees always named the oldest or youngest son after his grandfather: Joseph Peter, Peter Joseph, Joseph Peter. Then me: Patti Kay. I was supposed to be a Peter, though my parents could have given one of my two older brothers that name. Perhaps they were convinced they'd have more boys, not the six daughters and two sons they ended up with.

"That little tub's where we all took a bath," Dad tells me. I know the story, but I listen again. "Ma heated water on the stove for our Saturday night bath in the kitchen. When we got older, my ma talked my pa into getting a bigger galvanized tub. Joey's got that one in his garage."

I make out the faded sticker—"exclusive longer life coating." Some of that surely rubbed off on Dad. Why do I want this family relic so much? I live in a smallish house and bring home only what I can put to everyday use. I have no idea what I will do with this washtub, but I know I must have it.

"Take whatever else you want out there," Dad says.

Until my mom got sick, Dad didn't talk much. For most of their sixty-five years together, Mom's constant chatter drowned out anything he might have had to say. When Alzheimer's took her voice, Dad finally talked. For the last ten years, like a radio dial tuned to another station, he's been offering us daily news reports and other in-depth stories from throughout his life.

At home, I set my new treasure on top of my waist-high hot tub to scrub away decades of dirt. While I'm hosing it down, I can't help but think of the size difference between this two-foot-by-two-foot metal tub and my three-person jetted spa: a clear example of the excesses enjoyed by my generation. I soak in a pool of hot water with my husband just for fun.

This tub was used on my grandparents' farm for washing clothes and bodies from 1924 to 1935, give or take. Then it spent perhaps another fifteen years in the barn, occasionally brought out to hold ice and beer or to make ice cream in the summer. Was that when Grandpa Pete wrote his name on the tub? Did he loan it out to neighbors?

My grandparents moved to town around 1950, to a house with indoor plumbing. The tub moved with them. Was it filled with grandchildren's toys? Was it a vegetable bin? At some point, it was handed down to my dad, before or after his father died. Then it was stored in Dad's garage rafters for as long as I can remember, holding only he knows what. Camping gear? Strings of tangled Christmas lights?

I'd like to think Dad was drawn to this artifact's story, as I am, though most likely back then, he took anything his father offered

him for his own garage—Dad's domain. He built it himself in
1967, the year before I was born. For most of my life, he escaped
there to tinker or fix or just get away from a nagging wife and
eight boisterous kids. This washtub was stored there till Saturday
when Geralynn and I found it, along with a thousand Styrofoam
plates still in their wrappers. Before Dad retired as yardmaster of
the Soo Line Railroad, he had lunch each weekday with Amoco
Plastics factory workers, all of whom are now long gone. For my
dad, nearly everyone he once knew is gone. Even our Avon lady
is dead.

Scrubbing this tub, I can't help but say out loud: "Adults bathed
in this?" I imagine my grandparents' lean bodies during those
Depression years on the farm when they birthed four children
in five years. Babies and toddlers, two at a time, soaked in this
tub the size of a beer cooler. In the winter, it was surely placed in
front of the wood-burning kitchen stove. In the summer, it was
out in the grass, just on the edge of the fields. The youngest child
bathed first, then more hot water was poured from the tea kettle,
another child, more water. I see now: a family tradition.

I scrub and think of Dad's story: how he once farted during a
bath, and his older brother Jim cried because he did not want to
dip even a toe into that same water. Their mother, who carried a
leather strap on her apron to punish naughty boys or maybe just
for crowd control, refused to give Jim new water. He went two
weeks without a bath. Jim was called Jimmy then, and Dad was
Joey—"Irish twins" born fifty-three weeks apart.

Uncle Jim died a month ago. He was buried with the steel
ring he cherished since the autumn day when he met a girl selling
them from a ring-toss booth at a church picnic. He was married
to her for sixty-eight years. I didn't know this story till I read his
obituary, but I do know the key to a beloved's heart is sometimes

small and round. I wonder if he ever told any of his nine children about their Uncle Joe farting in the bathwater.

Scrubbing this tub, I feel like I do when I change my dad's sheets each Saturday morning. It's something about performing these domestic duties of women who came before me: washing whatever needs washing and unfurling crisp sheets upon a bed, knowing it's a treat on Saturday night to climb into clean sheets with a clean body.

I strip Dad's bed, and I swear I can smell my mother—a hint of Avon rose water—in their wool blankets. She's been dead four years now.

I am always struck by the tininess of their built-in double bed. No box spring, just a wooden platform and headboard Dad crafted by hand in 1955. Two adults and sometimes two children fit in this bed. I was one of them, sleeping in the small space between my parents' pillows and the headboard. I didn't have my own bed then; I just floated from room to room, a child with the ability to fit in spaces no one over age five could possibly squeeze into, like a bat or a mouse.

Someday soon, I won't have a father. Will I be a fifty-something orphan? Simultaneously, I wonder if my son will ever preserve my life as I have done with my parents' relics or if my things will be passed along, like those abandoned family photos you see in antique stores. Whatever we do to stave off that quickening heartbeat—like eat our raw veggies and give up smoking—we're still reminded: "I'm dying, too." That knowledge is ancient and deep and unavoidable.

I turn back to my project at hand. This washtub smells only of metal: the steely strength of lug nuts and blood. I scrub away the grime of my father's garage and the remnants of my kin's DNA. What remains are traces of stories none of us knows we leave behind.

No Green Bananas

Three months after Dad's bone cancer diagnosis, he goes off his pain meds to see if he really needs them. Why would a ninety-three-year-old worry about opioid addiction? Because he watches the news. After a day, his pain is so intense he can barely walk.

Now his plan is to take a pill every six hours, starting at five o'clock each morning. He needs an alarm clock.

"Get me the yellow one next to my bed," he tells me. "Please." I bring his clock radio, a gift from one of his eight kids in the 1980s, maybe me.

"No." I bring a small white one I used in grade school.

"No. Yellow," he barks. He's crabby today, which means he's in pain. I ask, "How are you feeling?"

"Fine," he grumbles.

"If you can't walk, we can't keep you home," I say gently. We've had this conversation before.

He looks straight ahead. "I know."

I am the one to whom he can show his anger and frustration. If he needs anything, he calls me. If something funny happens, or another relative dies, he calls me. This is an honor, though some days also a weight.

Today, I bring groceries. I won't joke about nearly putting back his bananas: too green for a nonagenarian with cancer. I finally

bring him the right alarm clock, one from his working days—
three decades ago—with the old-fashioned pin you pull to set
it. I put his alarm on the side table next to his lift chair, where he
spends close to twenty hours a day. He can't climb into his bed
anymore.

"Not yellow," I say, "but I bet this is the one you want?" This
dingy alarm was probably white in 1959, back when he had a four
thirty wake up each morning for his job at the Soo Line Railroad. I
plug it in. The cord is most likely a fire hazard, but I don't have the
patience for that battle right now. And it barely reaches this table.

"You're not going to be able to hear it," I say.

"Yes, I will."

"Maybe we can get an extension cord, so at least you can pick
it up and turn it off when you're in your chair. Or we can put it
on the other side?"

"It's fine as it is."

"You won't be able to see it."

"Don't worry about it." His tone is testy.

I set the alarm for five o'clock and pull the pin. Having this
relic in my hands, all I can think about is how he pulled the pin
out at bedtime and then pushed the pin in before dawn, marking
the time as his life passed by.

Pull the pin and lie there. Carry one baby to the crib, come
back and make another.

Push the pin in. Work twelve hours. Wolf down supper. Yell
at a kid—"You should be ashamed of yourself," a line Dad likely
learned from his own father—then drive to Boy Scouts or a
church meeting or both. Take another kid to basketball practice.
Pick one up from choir.

Pull the pin and lie there. Contemplate the house taxes coming due, sick kids, how to pay for another daughter's wedding.
Your mortality is years away.

Did Dad pull the pin like a fire extinguisher or like a grenade? I'll never know. We talk about grocery store ads and pain levels, about another dead guy with a too-long obituary.

~

I teach first-year university students, and when I cover life management, I show two ways of looking at time—lowercase and uppercase—with film clips from *Dead Poets Society*. "The first twenty problems at the end of Chapter One are due tomorrow," drones an unnamed chemistry teacher—an example of time. "Make your lives extraordinary," urges Robin Williams as the English teacher Mr. Keating—an example of Time. While some eighteen-year-olds may not understand, my hope is that some will.

Writer Annie Dillard says more about that balance between daily life and a lifetime: "How we spend our days is, of course, how we spend our lives. What we do with this hour, and that one, is what we are doing. . . . A schedule is a peace and a haven set into the wreck of time. . . . Each day is the same, so you remember the series afterward as a blurred and powerful pattern."

I can hear Dad's ancient clock. Its annoyingly loud ticking is something only a partially deaf man could sleep through. He says, "I want my alarm set for the morning. Don't pull the pin." He's impatient; I'm messing with his project.

The next day, a blizzard keeps me home. I call Dad to tell him I'm waiting to be plowed out. He hears best when his phone is set to speaker, so my voice fills his living room and reverberates back to me.

"How'd your alarm work?" I shout from my own living room five miles away.

He chuckles. "Well, I tell you what. Not so good. You put it by my bad ear. I couldn't hear it."

That's a surprise, I don't say. "Did you get your pain pill on time?"

"I woke up on my own. The alarm went off, but it didn't wake me."

I say, "With an extension cord, we can put the clock on the side with your good ear." When did I get to be such a fixer?

"Yeah, let's try that later," he says. I can hear in his voice: he's feeling better. "I put my clock in a metal pan."

I laugh. He explains, "When I was in my little cabin, I slept through my alarm so many times I was afraid I'd get fired. I put that alarm clock in a tin pie plate back then so I'd hear it better. I tried it last night."

I laugh some more at Dad's trick from 1947. "That's genius," I say. "I still think you should try the clock radio. You can turn the radio up as loud as you want. That will wake you. We could set it to the polka station."

My husband mouths: "He'll wake up dancing."

I say to Dad, "Bruce says to tell you if you use the clock radio, you could wake up dancing." In my head I hear "Beer Barrel Polka," one of Dad's favorites: "We've got the blues on the run."

Dad chuckles some more. "Yeah, I guess I could."

Sometimes dealing with my father is like interacting with a stubborn twelve-year-old. He needs to figure things out on his own. Sometimes it's like caring for a three-year-old who's dopey and charming. There's such a ferocious love between us that I want to stop time. But there's no pin to push or pull for that.

Everything Must Go

My father lived at 617 Harding Street in Chippewa Falls from 1953, the year he and my mother bought it as an unfinished one-and-a-half-story house, until his death in 2019. When he died at age ninety-three, he left behind about five tons of relics, including three floors of furniture from ten decades, 120 bud vases, more than 200 eight-track tapes, vintage Jim Beam decanters, a sauerkraut crock, and a thousand Amoco Christmas plates still in their original packaging.

Ten days before Dad died, he asked me, "You won't get a dumpster, will you?" He teared up. Dying was inevitable; his real sadness came from leaving his house and his things.

I teased, "The only reason we'd get one is because it would be so fun for me to dig your stuff out of it." My parents were collectors who filled every inch of every room. Their kids run the gamut from borderline hoarders, like a few of my five sisters and me, to neatniks like my two brothers.

Dad taught me to dumpster dive. Neither of us could ever drive past a free sign or even some items at the curb. I currently have ten mismatched dining chairs in my garage—part of my personal mission to keep perfectly good pieces out of the landfill even if I have no plan for them.

Dad was an American picker long before there was a TV series—at auctions in his younger years and at thrift sales during his last twenty-five years. He once got a great deal on twenty-eight pairs of his dead neighbor's underwear. My standards are a bit higher.

In "When You Die, I'll Be There to Take Your Stuff," the essayist Shane Cashman writes about his experiences working for an estate appraiser: "You learn a lot about a dead man rifling through his house—lifting his furniture, clearing his walls, going through his closets, finding out which psalms are dog-eared in his Bible—searching for anything that might be worth selling at auction. It feels like trespassing." Cashman laments that he clears out homes of the dead until there is no trace of them.

The longer we live, the more things we amass. Recently, that abundance has led to big business. One in eleven Americans pays for storage space, what one critic calls the "overflow of the American dream," at an average cost of ninety dollars per month.

Dad didn't believe in wasting money. Besides, he had three floors and a two-car garage with rafters; he made his own storage unit.

Currently, there are more than fifty thousand storage facilities in the United States, which offer a total of about 2.3 billion square feet of space to rent. One creative reporter calculated that the volume of these self-storage units could fill the Hoover Dam twenty-six times over. What happens to this excess after death? It's often auctioned off to bidders hoping to discover a suitcase of gold coins or a two-million-dollar Superman comic.

Dad's best treasures were divided among his children, grandchildren, and great-grandchildren—add in our partners and we're a crew of sixty-five. Then we held an estate sale, and a week later gave the rest away in a two-hour free-for-all from Dad's garage.

On the last day of our July sale, we took a break inside Dad's air-conditioned house, and my family and I sang happy seventieth to our oldest sister. Hers was the last See birthday we will ever celebrate at 617 Harding. Even the timbre of our voices sounded different in the empty rooms. Soon enough, we knew, another family would live there.

As my parents were erased from their house, they appeared in mine. Dad's framed 4-H art project from when he was seven and the deer horns he taxidermied when he was fifty-seven now hang in my bathroom. In my hallway, I recently mounted the original wooden house number sign he took down when he put on vinyl siding forty years ago. I'll always have 617 with me.

On the first Saturday in August, we arrange for Sofas for Service, a local veterans organization, to pick up Dad's furniture and three vacuums just before our mass giveaway. Even while volunteer Pete and his partner load up their truck, cars line the street in waiting.

Once I put up our free sign, the feeding frenzy begins, one Dad would have loved to watch. He liked a bargain, but free was always better. Someone immediately grabs our "family tuxedo," which I last wore trick-or-treating in 1981. One thirty-something fills a bag with music cassettes. "My grandpa is into tapes," he tells me.

"Then you should take a few more," I say.

People are shy. More than one person asks, "This is really all free?"

Across the street, two entrepreneurial siblings, ages five and six, notice the crowd and set up a folding table to sell ice cold lemonade for a nickel. I sit in the shade and watch our customers carry their loads of freebies to cars, then beeline to the kids. Soon their price shoots up to twenty-five dollars a cup, until their mom comes out to set them straight about the cent and dollar signs.

A guy picks up Dad's chimney sweep, which looks like a fancy metal lantern. I walk toward him just to ask, "What are you gonna do with that?"

He says, "Use it in one of the fountains I build."

"A chimney sweep?"

He shows me photos on his phone: a bed frame rigged onto stilts behind a three-tiered water feature with scavenged scrap metal scattered throughout the rock. Bizarre and perfect. Who would giggle most at this? Dad.

A woman cradles five VHS tapes and an adult toilet topper, Dad's "throne." This pairing makes me smile. If Dad was here, I'd joke, "Guess what she's gonna do when she gets home?" And he'd shoot back, "I can't believe some people have a TV and a tape player in their bathroom." These past four months, I've had plenty of conversations with my dead father.

A stranger says to me, "Sorry for your loss, girl." Her voice is filled with kindness. She's here because she saw my Craigslist ad: "Everything must go. Our dad didn't want his 93 years' worth of treasures going in a dumpster. Come take anything for free."

Dad may live on forever in some rural water feature or for a much shorter time with the dude who took a box of his half-used shampoos and lotions. I'll realize later that all of these strangers—who grab Dad's faded bath towels and sheets, his plaid shirts and slippers, his toy trucks and mixing bowls—are part of my family's grieving process as we give our father away piece by piece.

Cribbage Family

Like many Chippewa kids, I perfected my counting skills playing cribbage: "15-2, 15-4, 15-6, and six more is a doz." As the youngest of eight, I could only compete with siblings two or three times my age in games like 500 Rummy, sheephead, and cribbage. We sometimes saw black-and-white photos of the Kennedys playing football on the rambling front lawn of their Hyannis Port estate. The Sees moved dirty dishes and heaping ashtrays to one side of the kitchen table and played cribbage in our cramped Chippewa Falls home.

One day, during the summer I turned nine, I was playing my older brother and winning by a huge margin. Did I have a "perfect twenty-nine" cribbage hand, four fives and a jack, the highest possible score in one deal? Let's say I did, and I was little-sister loud about it. It's called skunking when you win by thirty-one points or more. I don't remember our exact exchange, but I am sure I was a haughty winner, a character flaw I still recognize in myself.

Down the homestretch, did I yell "Skunk!"? Let's say I did. My brother, having had enough, slapped my face. My Juicy Fruit flew across the room. I instantly started to wail, more from surprise than anything. Mom came running from the kitchen. I plumped out my lip in her direction and pointed to my gum on the shag carpet. Five-foot-nothing Mom stormed toward my gangly teen brother, screaming into his chest. He ran out the back door and squealed away in Dad's boat-like Chevy Impala. I cried harder at such big drama. Nothing like this happened before or since, which is why I still laugh about it.

This Saturday night, Bruce and I have a drink and play on a board my father made for me when I got married the first time, now a thirty-year-old relic. Dad crafted cribbage boards out of scraps he picked from the trash, wood from a neighbor's fallen tree, or existing boards from thrift sales that he repurposed by covering up "Las Vegas" or "Wisconsin Dells" with his own painted alphabet noodles and shellac. Many of his boards seem like works of folk art now, family heirlooms even. Others are still gag gifts. Unlike nineteenth-century Inuits, who fashioned cribbage boards from walrus tusks, Dad made some of his out of used toilet seats. He scavenged neon pegs from old Lite Brites, something Sir John Suckling, British poet and gambler, could not have imagined when he invented cribbage early in the 1600s. Settlers brought the game from England to America. Originally played primarily by men, cribbage in Wisconsin has intersected with the family tavern, with camping and dorm rooms, and more recently with coffee shops and microbreweries. As always, it's cheap, fun, and easily portable.

Tonight, as I count my cribbage hand, I say playfully to Bruce, "Hmmph. Twenty-one points. Is that all?"

He teases, "Think I could get your brother to come over and teach you a lesson?" Point taken loud and clear: sore losers are bad, but poor winners are worse.

Years into my mother's Alzheimer's diagnosis—when she couldn't even count coins—Dad still took her to cribbage tournaments every Saturday at a rural tavern called Four Corners (now Joel's 4Corners). One time, in the midst of a round against rival partners, she asked Dad, "Have I played this game before?" He nodded. "This is fun," she exclaimed. They went on to win the tournament, all muscle memory on her part. Did the competition wonder if my parents' strategy was an octogenarian shakedown? No one would have known that, for this old man, playing cribbage with his wife made life seem almost normal—made it seem like maybe she wasn't really slipping away.

When climbing stairs made it too challenging for Dad to leave home, he played cribbage for money with his friend Wayne, who showed up at Dad's twice a week for four years. The two of them swapped the same seven bucks back and forth up until Dad died six months ago.

～

I don't recall teaching my twenty-eight-year-old son to play cribbage, which means he likely learned the way I did: from watching.

One April morning, I get the second-worst phone call a parent can receive: accident, brain bleed. The worst call is a dead child; I am shocked but hopeful as I book a flight to Texas and pack within minutes. Out of habit, I throw in my travel cribbage board, as necessary as a toothbrush when I leave home. Twelve hours later, I exit my last plane and spot a uniformed police officer at the end of the ramp. This is it: my son is dead. I steady myself on the railing. The officer immediately speaks of Alex in the present tense and rushes me to his trauma unit room.

Alex's face is unrecognizable: purple eyelids puffed shut, alien head swollen twice its size and wrapped in a blood-stained bandage. Only my son's nose is familiar to me. When a doctor explains Alex's skull fracture, I visualize an egg cracking on a curb. But unlike Humpty Dumpty, Alex will heal.

On that trip, the cribbage board lay in my bag for days, a talisman, a reminder of better times. A few weeks later, I visit after Alex's release from a traumatic brain injury rehabilitation center. I bring along one of Dad's homemade cribbage boards he chose just for his grandson, all sleek wood and perfectly drilled holes. Alex and I play at his kitchen table, late on a Saturday afternoon.

I am on high alert: what skills has he lost? Can he still under-stand the complexities of this game? Of life? Part of Alex's rehab homework is doing Sudoku and reading, both of which he breezes through but hates. Cribbage is fun—not really a test.

Ten minutes into our first round, I'm about twenty-five points ahead. How can I skunk a guy with a head injury? I try not to fixate on the twelve-inch incision on the top of his head, like stitching on a baseball, a lifesaving "bone flap" where surgeons cut his skull apart to relieve pressure on his swelling brain. I want to throw the game, but I'm getting the best hands ever.

Alex slowly comes from behind, whooping at me as he passes my red peg with his green one, counting out loud dramatically. His East Coast roommate comes down to see our Wisconsin family ruckus. I take it all in: my slow demise on this cribbage board—a treasure made by my father, one my son might someday play on with his own kids, Alex's lightning-quick counting, and his wise moves to beat me.

He's gonna be okay, says a voice in my head. *My son is really gonna be okay.*

Goodbye 617

In 1953, Joe and Virgie See and their three preschool daughters were living in a one-bedroom cold-water Chippewa Falls apartment when they bought a house at 617 Harding Street for seven thousand dollars. Even with its unfinished basement and attic, this 1,800-square-foot one-and-a-half story must have seemed like a castle to my parents. They brought five more children home to 617 in 1954, 1956, 1958, 1961, and 1968. I was the last to arrive and the last to leave.

The eight of us kids shared toys and bikes and lumpy beds, sometimes three at a time. We shared one three-channel rabbit-eared TV in the living room (which Mom called the "front room") and one black rotary-dial telephone. Though we spanned nineteen years, we all learned to read from the same first-grade teacher at Holy Ghost Grade School, Mrs. Florence Krumenauer, and at McDonell High School, we all learned to type from Sister Paul Marie. We were constantly called by one another's names at home and at school. We wore one another's clothes and shoes, ate off of one another's plates, and said mean and funny and kind words to one another. We helped one another with homework and outfits, with breakups, and with the deaths of our parents. All at 617 Harding.

After Dad died last spring, we cleaned out the house. Each of us took our own eleven-by-fourteen framed first communion picture, which felt a little like breaking up the band. This set of eight pictures adorned the front-room wall for years, a focal point that visitors were drawn to and regulars expected. We six girls looked downright angelic in the same lacy dress and veil; the two boys wore sport coats with rosary-draped hands. That day dividing treasures, all of us—ages fifty-one to seventy—posed in front of the bare wall and held up these ghost portraits, a Catholic-school-style "before and after," as if we reached back through time to reclaim our second-grade selves.

◆

Over the next few months, we emptied out 617, then painted and polished and put it on the market.

This past Christmas, the homing device in my heart kicked in: I drove to Mom and Dad's.

Once inside, I walked from room to empty room. I opened every door and drawer. I peered in at Dad's last few groceries none of us wanted to take away. Hamburger in the freezer and Leinenkugel's in the fridge would mean someone still lived there. I took the lid off his last tin of coffee and found his metal measuring spoon. I slipped it in my pocket, a gift on that lonely first Christmas day without him.

Dad's kitchen counter—where we usually set up crockpots filled with holiday ham and cheesy potatoes and calico beans—was covered with realtors' cards. I didn't yet know that yesterday's counteroffer had been accepted.

I thought about the three generations of babies welcomed into that house. I was conceived there; twenty-two years later, so was my son.

I thought about the laughing and yelling and swearing that went on at 617, the slammed doors and the lullabies, all the dancing in the kitchen, all the kissing and hugging—hello, goodbye, please stay—that occurred on both sides of the back door. The phrases rushed through my head like a love song for 617.

I thought about all the suppers we wolfed down so we might be the first to get seconds. Every kid touched every piece of chicken to find the right one, and we fought over the heart and gizzard even though half of us didn't care. We retold stories and jokes until they were as familiar as our worn dining table.

I thought about all the parties at 617. Card parties, neighbor parties, birthday and holiday parties, backyard and garage parties that streamed into the house after dark. Or the party for one my father held each night when he escaped to his basement den, brandy old-fashioned in hand, woodstove roaring, *M*A*S*H* reruns blaring, Mom shouting from the top of the stairs, "How many drinks did you have?"

He always called back, "Two." She would tease him: "You can't count past two."

In the empty basement, I considered how this interaction embodied their relationship. I thought about Dad's whistling, his wet pucker and shrill off-key tune—something from last Sunday's mass or an eight-track tape he scored at a thrift sale—that filled this house after every fight and meant "all is okay."

Two people couldn't be together for seven decades without a little dysfunction. Nor could a family as large as ours not endure fallouts and feuds. I thought about one of Anne Lamott's "12 Truths I Learned from Life and Writing": "Families are hard, hard, hard, no matter how cherished and astonishing they may also be."

I was sitting in my Subaru in Dad's driveway, metal spoon in hand, when a sister pulled up. Geralynn shares my homing device. Neither of us could say how our grief that day felt like wearing a cement overcoat. Instead, we chatted through her open car window.

～

On January 18, a week before 617 is officially sold, my family gathers at Holy Ghost Church—what Dad loved calling "Holy Goat." This would have been his ninety-fourth birthday. Mass is being offered in Dad's name, and afterward we're having a party.

I feel close to Dad, nestled into the "See pew" where he sat every Sunday for almost seventy years. I think about all the hours he volunteered at this parish and school, all of the See baptisms and first communions and confessions, the confirmations and weddings he witnessed here for his kids and some of his sixteen grandkids and twenty great-grandkids—a family that grew to sixty-five bodies.

Then my mind turns to Dad's favorite church joke, which should never be told or even thought about in church.

Later that night at my brother's, I tell it to my siblings and their spouses in the same voice Joe See would have used: "So anyway, this guy walks in to work on Monday with two black eyes." Some are hearing Dad's joke for the first time. The punchline is an old groaner. Still, I laugh until I cry.

The night before we close on the house, I walk through one last time. Our DNA may live on at 617: sloughed-off skin or a strand of hair caught in a drawer. Still, for good measure, I add in permanent marker "The Sees, 1953–2020" on an attic beam hewn by my father's hands—solid, enduring, ours.

Firebugs

"You play with fire, you'll wet the bed." When I was a kid, my mom said this to me nearly each time we had a campfire. Recently, I Googled her phrase; turns out this warning is used around the world, generally to keep children from playing with matches. For the record: I never peed myself. At least, not after playing with fire.

Campfire, woodstove, gas fireplace, or candle—I am entranced by any flame. I've been called "firebug" by parents, friends, and a husband or two. One sister even calls me a pyromaniac. Doesn't everyone like to observe the different types of ignition, say, when a dried squirrel's nest flares versus a smoldering fifty-year-old toilet seat?

I love to burn. As a teen, I poked dripping candles with paper-clips or knives just to watch the wax flow, and I held strands of hair and sweater fuzz over flames to see that quick poof.

Whenever we camped, Mom made popcorn over the fire with an old pot filled with that morning's bacon grease and yellow kernels. Only a firebug could stand that heat and smoke the way she did, squatting dangerously close to the blaze with just a charred oven mitt on her hand, shaking the pan until popcorn spilled over. I'll always love the scent of burning pine logs mixed with the aroma of Mom's snack. The perimeter of our campsite flickered with fireflies, like sparks blown into the woods.

Fires have always soothed me. As my parents lay dying—seven years apart—I handled my grief the same way: I'd come home from sitting with them and burn in my yard. I'd stare at the flames, primeval and comforting, and process my day. Science supports that the sight, sounds, and smells of a fire lower blood pressure and induce relaxation.

Fires are a communal experience. Fueled by flames and often drinks, I have listened to and confessed secrets, told endless stories, and shared recaps of even the dullest aspects of life. Fires allow us to fixate on the blaze, so even the most mundane or embarrassing thing can be said without eye contact.

For our Stone Age ancestors, fire meant safety, survival, and eventually socializing. Flintstones to Jetsons: today Tesla cars offer the option of a flickering fire video on the dashboard screen, or you can download a fire app on your smartphone for a little romantic ambiance.

In *Castaway*, Tom Hanks's marooned character builds a fire by rubbing sticks on dry weeds. He screams out to no one: "Look what I have created: I have made fire." I feel this accomplishment each time I gaze into a fire of my own making.

～

At the end of March, I build a huge one from wood scraps and months of unrecyclable food containers. My phone rings: my across-the-lake neighbor, Larry. As a hello, I say, "You like my fire, don't you?"

He says, "There's a burn ban on."

"Whaaat?" I whine.

"I don't want you to get in trouble. It started yesterday."

I say, "Well I guess now you get to see me put out a beautiful fire." Larry laughs.

Four buckets of sand and water finally douse it. All the while, I grumble to myself that Larry could have called before he watched me light this fire.

I had never built a bonfire in winter until I moved to Lake Hallie. At the first fire-on-ice party my husband and I hosted, one of my brothers brought along a few gallons of cooking oil left over from his many fish fries. He periodically doused the fire with an accelerant that made everyone *ooh* and *aah* and crave french fries.

My other brother fashioned two slim pokers into a grabber, which my son used to arrange burning wood. No one gave instructions; we just acted out a well-orchestrated, silent fire dance. My nephew set frozen logs around the perimeter—drying fuel on deck. Mitch makes a fire outside his Northside Eau Claire home a few times a week, no matter the season. "Anything burns if you get the fire hot enough," he told me once.

That night, my husband asked the small crowd, "Are all of you firebugs?" My family members chuckled; no one had to say that singed eyebrows and leg hair are rites of passage for the Sees.

This was the first time Bruce saw us in action: less like a NASCAR pit-stop team changing a tire—as you might guess if you knew us—and more like a ballet troupe.

Years ago, on the first couples trip Bruce and I took with Tiit and Ann Raid, I discovered another fellow firebug. I should have known: Tiit's December birthday parties often featured a mammoth bonfire outside his Fall Creek home.

That trip, Tiit and I realized we both wanted a hand in the fire. I teased, "Age before beauty." I watched in awe as he designed a structure and lit it with one match. He perfected his skill during the summers he and Ann went on June-to-August "working vacations" in their tricked-out 1968 Dodge van. He was on break from teaching art at the University of Wisconsin–Eau Claire, and Ann would quit whatever job didn't allow her time off. They traveled the country and landed odd jobs: picking berries in Washington or making candles in Colorado. Each night, Tiit constructed a campfire, often in a different design—traditional log cabin or teepee—that ignited with one spark.

This summer, the few cool nights mean campfires for Bruce and me. One dusk in mid-August, Bruce spots a firefly beyond the glow of our fire. I've always felt a kinship: I am drawn to any flame, and lightning bugs are drawn to the flames of one another. Last year, we regularly saw only one in our yard—so sad because their language of light is a mating call.

Bruce and I again reminisce that when we were children, even city yards twinkled with more fireflies than a kid could count. Reduction of habitat and light pollution mean fewer fireflies all over the world. Unlike other insects and animals who move on when their land is overrun by human progress, fireflies just die.

I don't care that they're really beetles, and if I saw one in daylight, I would want to squash it. I still squawk with joy each time I see one at night. Now we spot another and another. I stop counting after twenty. A love fest right here in our yard, where they have dead logs for their larvae and access to water and long grass.

We watch two particularly amorous fireflies signal in a constant call and response. One blinks her neon sign: "Wanna dance?" And tonight, thankfully, it's not followed by dark silence.

Nothing Happened
or Everything Did

The view from the author's house on Lake Hallie. PHOTO BY BRUCE TAYLOR

For All the Handy Men
I've Loved

This Valentine's Day, I'm remembering all the handy men I've loved: those who fixed that squeak and settled that threshold and rewired that lamp. Anyone who looked around a room and said, "What's this—about ten by twelve?" then shot a tape measure out of his hand like Spiderman slinging a web and measured exactly ten by twelve.

This is for my father, who sketched out plans for his sister-in-law's farmhouse, then helped build it with no formal training other than trial and error. This is for my brother Dave, who at age sixteen helped Dad turn our basement into a family room and then, years later, remodeled his own house. For my brother Joe, who made his living as a home-builder and whose own home and cabin are perpetually under construction. For my crafty brothers-in-law. And for my son, who fashioned a bar and chairs from scavenged pallets.

This is for Don Knoll and all of his big ideas. Decades ago, when I hired him to paint my third-story window frames, he scanned my house and pitched, "I'd knock out this wall to give you a better spot for your fridge." Don always had work. He once told me that doing projects for single gals was like having twelve wives. I said since he was *paid* to take care of honey do lists, he never had to deal with the honey don'ts. He thought for a moment, then let out a husky laugh. We lost Don to cancer three years ago. I can't look at the screen porch he built without thinking of him.

This is for Jim Seymour, who lived around the block from me in Eau Claire and stopped by before or after his bigger jobs. He loved old houses and helped nudge my 1876 beauty into the twenty-first century. As his business grew and I moved away, I didn't call him for piddly things like changing a twenty-five-foot-high light bulb in the yard. But I wanted to.

I can handle a hammer, screwdriver, and drill. I can paint, decoupage, or cement over most surfaces, which is to say: I have vision. A few years ago, I researched how to transform our under-the-cupboard lazy Susan into a drawer. Every time I turned the dang thing, my potato chips slipped to the back and got stuck. Sometimes, I found the bag six months later.

I hired Mike Sabo. Though his first love is making jewelry, Mike can fix just about anything. He sipped a cup of coffee with my husband at our Lake Hallie kitchen counter, and I showed him a picture of the refitted drawer. He eyed the price. "Explain to me why you want to do that."

"So my chips don't go stale," I said.

"I'd just eat them faster," he told me. Bruce gave a nod to Mike's handyman wisdom. Neither had to say, "Well, if it ain't broke . . ." I still have that lazy Susan; I store my snacks elsewhere. And Mike's aches and pains got the better of him. He doesn't hire out his services anymore.

I married a man who is quite handy whenever I need the perfect verb for a sentence, and he taught me how to end my essays so they close like a perfectly made box. Bruce knows his strengths. I tell him he's not alone: a recent survey shows that 40 percent of American men reported they either can't do anything around the house or they'd prefer to call a handyman. Bruce says, "The others lie." There's still a societal pressure for all guys to be fixers.

Bruce suspects more men in 2021, like him, would rather write a check and let someone else get his hands dirty.

Even the Gospel of Luke proclaims "the laborer is worthy of his hire." Apparently, my father never read that passage. Throughout six decades, he remodeled every room in his house—and the bathroom three times. At age seventy-five, he replaced all of his windows, alone.

I'm sure there were disasters. When I was a kid, he glued down linoleum in the kitchen and then slid the refrigerator across it. This was the first time I heard a certain swear word pass Dad's lips as he sliced through the floor. I now utter that word in my yard each time I run over an extension cord with the lawn mower. Dad would always chuckle as he spliced it back together for me. The first time I mowed after Dad died, I thought, "Be careful, there's no one to fix your cord." Until now.

I'll call this reluctant handyman M. He works on his own projects, but he's not really sure about working on anyone else's. He also happens to be my nephew. And: I don't want to share him.

I text M., "I know you redid all the floors in your house. Want to do some of mine?" The pandemic has been especially hard on small business owners; this is the perfect winter to hire him.

M. texts back, "I'll take a look at your materials." Noncommittal, but interested.

When he shows up, he gets more interested as he talks through the process of exactly how to assemble my click-together cork plank. I'm not sure if he's explaining how I should do it or talking through how he'll do it himself. This is how my father approached every project. I can almost hear Dad's voice: "Well, what a guy should *really* do . . ."

M. is a thinker and a perfectionist, the ideal combination in a handyman. We discuss his payment. M. suggests an hourly wage, one I think is too low.

"This is skilled labor," I say. I offer him ten dollars more per hour. He shrugs. Apparently neither of us knows how negotiations usually play out.

A week later, M. lays the floor in my office. Afterward, I text a photo to his wife. "That's a great look. Can you give him more jobs?" she asks. I'm not sure if she's helping me or herself by keeping him busy.

Bruce points out that this is a little like wives making playdates for their husbands. I don't care. I make a list, wait a few days, and text M. about my other projects. "I can probably do that," he texts.

When M. comes back to cover a popcorn ceiling, I take down my dad's two-foot wooden level that I display over my office doorframe. This vintage tool reminds me how I want my life to be: smooth and balanced.

"That looks like Grandpa's," M. says.

I nod. I don't have to explain to this nephew—who learned construction from his father, who learned from mine—the satisfaction of doing good-enough work that when you lay a level and watch that bubble perfectly align, no matter what else has gone wrong in your life, for one moment, the world is plumb and true.

The Cruelest Month

After last February's record snowfall, I'm filled with more dread than usual about what the next twenty-eight days will bring. All of us who survived damaging ice dams are paranoid. Since November, I've been shoveling our roof edges with my twenty-five-foot snow rake. Drive around the Chippewa Valley, and you'll see evidence of the same patterns on roof after roof. Poet T. S. Eliot famously claimed, "April is the cruelest month." He never experienced February in Wisconsin.

I remember back when weather forecasters reported temperatures and windchills, and what they felt like was up to you. Now our smartphones tell us what the weather "feels like," and it's always worse than the actual temperature. At my most crotchety—usually in February—I wonder, "What snowflake meteorologist invented that?" We also constantly hear about the ominous polar vortex, which seems like a plot to make winters seem more frightening.

But a little research shows that winters *are* worse in Wisconsin (and across the United States). According to Climate Signals, a nonprofit science information project, "North America is the only place on Earth experiencing far-below-normal temperatures." One theory is that melting sea ice in the Arctic weakens the jet stream, which allows polar air to travel farther south than usual. This means average February temperatures in Cold Bay, Alaska, are now warmer than those in Green Bay, Wisconsin.

Director of the Atmospheric Sciences Program at the University of Georgia, Marshall Shepherd, reminds us that "weather" is what happens this week, while "climate" is what happens this year and beyond—a lesson many of us learned in fifth-grade science. Marshall, the former president of the American Meteorological Society, adds: "It is not 'Where You Live Warming,' it is 'Global Warming.'"

I know we should never say which winter is the worst, so let's just say some are more memorable than others. The first time our pipes froze and burst, February of 2012, my husband was home alone. Water gushed through ceiling tiles in the basement. Our shut-off valve is behind a removeable wall, a design flaw we had not discovered until this emergency. Bruce called our neighbor and fellow homebody Jerry Sabaska. These two retirees used to take turns liking each other's Facebook posts from across frozen Lake Hallie. They rarely left home in winter, so they were the perfect guys to call if you needed something.

Jerry thought for a moment, and then said, "Just kill the power to the well." When Jerry told me the story later, he laughed: "Bruce dropped the phone. He didn't even hang up."

A panicked Bruce ran down to turn off the breaker.

The second time a pipe burst, in February 2018, water leaked into a crawl space beneath the house. I cut the drywall out of our laundry room in the area where we heard spurting water and discovered the pipes were between the cement foundation and the insulation—the opposite of where they should be. No heat was getting to them, another sign our cabin was built as a three-season house. The former owner drained the pipes each fall and didn't give them another thought as she basked in the Florida sun all winter.

We tore out the drywall five feet up from the floor, creating a look I called redneck wainscoting. I stuffed insulation behind each pipe, my thin fingers barely able to push the quilting through. In May, those exposed pipes and tufts of pink and brown still remind us of our hardiness and the prize for surviving another February: glorious spring in Wisconsin.

Until our ice dams of 2019 (which resulted in water leaking directly over our bed), Bruce and I called 2018 the winter from hell. Weeks of freezing and thawing meant our steep driveway became a luge by February. No amount of salt and sand allowed us to drive our MINI Cooper up the quarter-mile hill to the road. AAA wouldn't tow it because technically we weren't stuck. Finally, I asked Jerry to pull our car to the top with his pickup truck and tow rope.

On my first day of trudging up the drive to a frozen car in subzero temperatures, I stopped my ascent and glanced at the beautiful scene below—sun coming up beyond Jerry and Helen Sabaska's house across the lake, lovely puffs of smoke curling out of their chimney. I eyeballed the distance from my dock to their back door: shorter than what I had just walked. I called to ask if I could park in their driveway.

That afternoon, when I dropped off the car, I went inside to leave my keys in case Jerry needed to move my vehicle to plow. He quizzed me about the MINI Cooper, as he has about every car I've driven since I was sixteen and his daughter's best friend. Thirty-three years later, I said confidently: "It's a four cylinder."

None of us knew that was Jerry's last winter. By August, he'd be dead.

"I could start your car in the morning," Helen offered. No uphill trek and a toasty car? Heavenly.

She reminded me that when she was a teen, she made a daily trip past my house to get from her farm at the north end of the lake to work at her family's dance hall on the other end (now the site of the Eau Claire Press Company).

"I walked up and down your driveway sometimes four times a day," she told me. She didn't mention the ninety-nine steps carved into the earth that led from the lakeshore up to the Hoot, though she did tell me her usual punchline: "I didn't have a weight problem back then."

The next morning, Helen calls me at 7:30. "Are you coming?"

"Just getting my gear on." That takes time for 18 degrees below zero. I'm wearing my dress clothes under wind-resistant sweatpants and three coats. Nanook of the North wore fewer layers. Only my eyes are visible.

With each crunching step across the frozen lake, I consider what Norwegians say: *Det finnes ikke dårlig vær, bare dårlige klær,* or "There's no bad weather, only bad clothing." It sounds more convincing in Norwegian, perhaps because it rhymes.

I walk up a slight incline to the Sabaskas' enclosed porch. Tall snowbanks mean the only way to access my car is through their house. Helen meets me at the sliding door: "I couldn't start your MINI."

"Is it dead?"

"I didn't remember how, and Jerry's asleep." The push button start is confusing. She would have failed her motor-head husband's car quiz.

I find Helen's plate of cookies on my passenger seat; they almost thaw by the time I get to work. This is what makes February bearable: neighbors you can rely on for whatever you need and, sometimes, for what you didn't even know you were missing.

Our Old Town

I stumbled upon the Facebook group Our Old Town Chippewa Falls just after its January launch. I wasn't hooked until Deb Stone posted a picture of her grandparents' Falls Drive-In where I car-hopped during the summers of 1984 and 1985. It was the first photograph I'd ever seen of this hangout from long ago. Back then, most of us did not have access to cameras—almost unimaginable now—and we would never have thought to take a picture of the place we called Tubbie's. At age fifteen, I carved my name into the red counter, joining thirty years of names etched on summer days by girls who played the same greasy radio in the same tiny kitchen or fitted trays to car windows. I sent Deb's photo to my two older sisters, who had worked there years before I did. Sharing these stories is what makes sites like Our Old Town Chippewa Falls (or Eau Claire or Wichita or Baltimore) so meaningful.

Five years ago, Rick Atkinson created the Facebook group Old Chippewa Falls, which focused on the history of the city. Its spin-off, Our Old Town, is composed of members' recollections and photographs, a free-for-all offering prompts that spark memories for Chippewa townies like me: "Remember Skogmo's or the Rumble Bridge?" Other prompts could apply to any townie anywhere: "Who was your favorite teacher?" or "What was the best sledding hill?"

"Chippewa will always be my hometown," Rick tells me. Like

many of us, he omits the *Falls*—one way natives like me spot other natives.

Our Old Town is frequented by almost three thousand current or former Chippewa residents. This is our own MeTV: like reruns of *The Andy Griffith Show* but featuring people with whom we're linked by only a few degrees of separation. My fellow travelers into the past take turns posing questions or simply throwing out names.

"Anyone go through the fence to get into the fair?" "The Hoot." "Miss Shipman, librarian." "Reiter's Steakhouse." "St. Charles custodian, a lady." "Sully's Bar."

Story after story follows. The writer in me wants to categorize: iconic places, memorable people, and old advertisements for things like Leino, which was Leinenkugel's breakfast drink brewed during Prohibition.

My childhood friend Sandy Boos Stephens posts about Van's Supper Club: "My dad and Baldy Gaier made a Vikings/Packers bet, and Baldy lost so he had to push my dad out to Van's in a wheelchair." She shares a Polaroid of them with her dad's handwritten caption: "One drunk & one dummy."

Like the rest of the world, I am hunkered down and looking for an escape from recent COVID-19 pandemic worries. I'm not alone in seeking comfort from memories, which connect and soothe us. A psychology professor at the University of Southampton, Dr. Constantine Sedikides, focuses her work on the science of nostalgia. From the Greek word *nostos*, which means homecoming, this state of mind often fills us with sentimentality for the past and counteracts anxiety and loneliness. "Nostalgizing" even brings on physical warmth, a glow, something we Wisconsinites can often use. Eau Claire writer John Hildebrand called nostalgia "an ache in the heart for what is unrecoverable" in his recent collection *Long Way Round: Through the Heartland by River*. At its core, the book is an examination of Wisconsinites' pull toward the past.

Our Old Town member Ronald Kranig asks for comments about classmates who have passed away. He writes, "Remember, a lot of us would not be what we are today without the friendship we had with these people." The list that follows is heartbreaking.

A person could write a full column, if not a book, on any of these posts.

"Remember when Robert Kennedy spoke at McDonell?" "Skateland." "Did anyone else go downtown on a Friday night with their parents and sit in the car to 'watch the people'?" "The Mill Pond."

Someone responds, "I remember the smell of the warming house." And another: "We practically lived there in the winter. Swam in the pond in the summer until dog days and polio season."

"Miss Kranzfelter from junior high," one member writes. "She was so short . . . she needed a stool to reach the blackboard." Someone adds, "She would point out such neat things like 'Can you see four colors in the sky?' "

Dr. Sedikides's work supports the theory that when we remember the past, we often become more optimistic about the future, as if nostalgia gives us the oomph and enthusiasm to keep moving forward. That idea is challenging for me to wrap my head around. If the present feels stagnant or overwhelming, do we tend to look to the past, which then helps us look forward to tomorrow? Maybe, as Hildebrand claims, "The only cure is to try something new."

Looking back with a tinge of longing can be healthy, but reminiscing about my favorite lunch lady doesn't mean I want to return to high school.

One Our Old Town member writes to me: "So many fun memories of simpler times, when family and friends were really REAL, and not counted up as in Facebook today." Those times may have been simpler, yes, but likely not better for most people. Back then, few laws prevented discrimination of any kind. Almost every home was blue with secondhand smoke and covered in lead paint. And don't get me started on the environment: our bald eagle population was nearly decimated in the 1960s and 1970s. If I posted these words on any Our Old Town site, I might be asked to take my "political" talk elsewhere.

Like other members, I want to remember gathering at Workman's Bar or eating pizza at Brothers Three. And I want to read about former Chippewa kids' memories of their good-time places.

Visual storyteller Dan Ritzinger posts a photo of his dad with friends outside of Emil's Hob-Nob, circa 1940, at the corner of Columbia and High Streets. Today, it's a parking lot. Tracy Savage posts a photo of her family in front of Babe's (now West Hill Bar), circa 1948. Her grandmother, Edith Duren, was Babe's sister. Tracy recalls, "My grandparents used to take us . . . and we got pop and potato chips—a real treat. We had to keep it a secret because my dad hated us going there."

I don't know most of the folks mentioned in these recollections, but I'm enthralled by each photo. The way Glen and the guys hold their beer bottles at different angles, how the late afternoon sun casts shadows upon each man. How Edith and the gals cluster with their children in front. And the stories we'll never know: why did they step out on the sidewalk for this happy hour or after-church pose?

I cannot do justice to these photographs with words. Seeing them for yourself is like experiencing the difference between reading about an ice-cold Leinie's and drinking one.

Perhaps especially now, many of us crave the community found in these posts: a middle-aged daughter missing her Vikings-loving dad, a grandmother recalling where she first learned to look for many colors in the sky, or simply the memory of old friends gathering together to have fun. Time pauses on Our Old Town Chippewa Falls, or perhaps it stops forever.

Shake-a-Day

The first pandemic-related shock for me came late in the afternoon on St. Patrick's Day 2020 when I heard that Wisconsin bars were closing. COVID-19 had loomed far away until then. Now, months later, there are bigger concerns: unprecedented loss of life and income, not to mention a group of deniers who don't believe in social distancing or mask-wearing despite the long-standing science that proves they are effective at slowing the spread of the virus. I love a conspiracy theory as much as anyone, and I appreciate having the freedom to go wherever I please. Still, I will not take chances to socialize. For many of us, staying home sometimes feels like house arrest, and we pine for the routine of going to work and to all of our other familiar spots.

In his book *The Great Good Place*, sociologist Ray Oldenburg wrote about the necessity of having a "third place." His subtitle—*Cafés, Coffee Shops, Bookstores, Bars, Hair Salons, and Other Hangouts at the Heart of a Community*—describes exactly what we miss throughout these chaotic times. Besides home (our first place) and work (our second place), our third places are our anchors to community life.

Looking back, I see that my third place has always been a bar. In the 1970s, Mom and Dad would load us kids in the car for a Sunday afternoon drive, usually caravanning with another family. The highlight was stopping at a tavern, often Jump River Rosie's about an hour away. The children ate Slim Jims, drank Orange Crush, and played pinball or air hockey with other kids. The parents shared a pitcher of Leinie's and took their turn at the Shake of the Day.

I sometimes sat on my mom's lap, banged that beat-up leather dice cup on the edge of the bar rail, and blew on the dice for luck as I'd seen my dad and countless other patrons do. To my little-girl mind, this was like Yahtzee: shake three times, try for five of a kind. Every buck paid to play went into the pot, or kitty. Winning meant whooping and hollering as the bartender counted out stacks of one dollar bills—and that was just how my parents celebrated, not to mention us kids. In our neck of the woods, we called it Shake-a-Day, something Mom loved so much we even mentioned it in her obituary.

In his article "How Bar Dice Became a Wisconsin Institution," Robert Simonson writes that the game is as widespread throughout the state as "over-the-top Bloody Mary garnishes and Brandy Old-Fashioneds." I'm more interested in bar people—that's what I love most about taverns. There's always something getting ready to happen, an unpredictable mix of characters and stories.

The last time I visited Lake Hallie Sportsman's Club, I trekked there on the frozen lake during halftime of the Badger men's basketball game. Along the way, I stopped to talk to families out for the Sportsman's Take a Kid Fishing contest. I remember that ordinary Saturday as extraordinary now. Strangers in groups, live basketball on TV. None of us could imagine that most public places soon would close because of the pandemic.

When I walked in, everyone turned to look. The regulars noticed I might not quite be one of them, but I probably resembled their sisters or wives. I talked about the game and the weather and the kids out fishing. For a few hours, I was a guest—no choosing sides on politics or most sports.

A guy called out to me, "You must be a See girl. How old are you?" Turned out he was my oldest brother's classmate. I sat on the stool beside him. As we talked, I discovered he was the brother of my high school crush and my dad's retired Roto-Rooter guy, connections that rarely surprise me anymore in Chippewa.

The bartender brought my Leinie's Light and said to Mark, "Really? You ask a woman her age before she sits down?" We all laughed.

Oldenburg claims a third place must be welcoming and comfortable—a place where you meet both new and old friends. That day, I was there for the shake. Sportsman's offered three types: Box Shake, Dollar Shake, and Fifty Cent Shake, each with a different pot. I lost at all of them. Mark bought me a beer.

Every barfly has a Shake-a-Day story. One guy told me he once won $2,400. "Right here?" I asked. Nothing is illegal, since bars don't profit from shakes aside from the rule that you have to buy a drink to play. Others tell about pots over ten thousand dollars, often at hole-in-the-wall places.

Jim Draeger, bar historian and coauthor of *Bottoms Up: A Toast to Wisconsin's Historic Bars and Breweries*, claims tavern dice began in our state around the end of Prohibition. Rules for winning are different from bar to bar: the bigger the pot, the more complex the game. Some use twelve-sided dice or require one shake to roll five or even ten dice of the same number. The odds of rolling five of the same number in one shake are 1 in 1,296. You can see why the kitty grows.

Many months ago, my husband and I spent a late afternoon Shake-a-Day-hopping along Highway OO, what Bruce has dubbed the Lake Hallie Strip: a little cheaper and perhaps seedier than the one in Vegas. Four bars, four shakes, all on a one-mile stretch.

At Hallie Bar, the bartender warns me that someone won the kitty earlier in the day, which means there's nothing left in the pot. Still, I pay her a dollar and try to roll as many threes as I can. I'm here doing research, after all. What a story if I win my own dollar back! I discover that some of the diviest bars have the nicest dice cups. This one feels like expensive leather gloves. The bartender says, "If you don't roll any threes, you get a free drink."

Maybe losers do prosper. "My kind of game," I say to Bruce. He watches cliff diving on one of the four TVs with a much-tattooed man whose voice lilts like he's perpetually telling a joke. I shake one three; I win nothing.

Oldenburg says that a third place is important not only to help a person establish a sense of home and a connection to their community but also for maintaining civility, civic engagement, even democracy. Pretty heady stuff for a tavern. No wonder I miss it now. In order to contain this pandemic successfully, we'll all have to be community minded, as if our lives depend upon it. For some of us, they do. As much as I love Shake-a-Day and everything else about taverns, some activities are still not worth the gamble.

Get Your Blue Mind On

Eight years ago, after watching the Packers in a bar, my son bid on a 1987 Sun Tracker pontoon boat. Let's just say Alex's judgment wasn't crystal clear. The twenty-four-foot party barge needed new seats, carpet, and motor. Alex finished college and military training, then landed a job in Texas, so his rebuilt beauty stayed behind in storage.

When my dad died in 2019, Alex rushed home for the funeral. Though he'd talked about selling his pontoon before, he was really ready this time. "Why don't you buy it," he pitched. "I'll give you a deal."

As much as I liked the thought of spending Dad's inheritance on a party barge lovingly restored by my son, I knew I had to float the idea past my husband. "What will we do with a boat that size on no-wake Lake Hallie?" Bruce asked. He finally agreed on the condition that we trade in the motor for a smaller one and name the pontoon after my dad.

Last summer, Minn Kota two-horsepower electric outboards were in high demand. We couldn't get one installed until August at Skeeter's, where Alex's boat had been wrapped in plastic since 2016. When we got it home, I stenciled on "The Jo Sea," a female aquatic version of Joe See. We christened her not with hoity-toity champagne but with Dad's favorite drink: a Mist and Mist, which is Canadian Mist and Sierra Mist.

That first week, we pontooned with all three of Bruce's kids, a rare treat. Dan drove, with Bruce beside him. Our new motor groaned and sputtered. I hit the switch to lift the trim. An ancient, mossy rope had choked the propeller. Noah climbed over the stern for a closer look. Former lifeguard Laura offered to jump in and pull us to the nearby landing. "Never get out of the boat," I said in my best *Apocalypse Now* impression.

Noah gave the rope a tug and joked about a dead body attached to it. Fortunately, Bruce doesn't go anywhere without a pocket knife. Noah sawed through the rope and freed the propeller. Anyone on shore that day may have heard a collective whoop of voices, boaters excited to be out together on that blue, blue day but even more thrilled that their party barge could take them home.

The original party barge cruised Lake Hallie one hundred and forty years ago, and it was actually a barge. The man-made lake was formed in 1843 and served as a nameless holding pond for a nearby sawmill called Blue Mills. When that mill was washed away in a flood, Badger Mills was built on the same site. And in 1891, as the logging industry waned, Badger Mills co-owner John Ure Jr. had a vision that Lake Hallie—which he named after his daughter—might become a recreational attraction. He christened his two steamboats after his other daughters: Loraine and Antoinette. One towed a barge on which couples danced as they sailed the lake.

I love to imagine how this must have looked: men swirling women in long dresses with bustles on a floating, fenced-in dance floor. The music from the Eau Claire City Brass Band playing on the deck of the steamboat likely carried for miles. Farmers looking up from their evening chores may have wondered if the source was insect or human.

People have forever been drawn to water. Wallace Nichols's book explains why. *Blue Mind: The Surprising Science That Shows*

How Being Near, In, On, or Under Water Can Make You Happier, Healthier, More Connected, and Better at What You Do is quite a title and a proclamation. Human brains are hardwired to react positively to water not only for its calming effects but also for water's ability to heal and even spark creativity. Nichols calls it "getting your blue mind on."

～

I was more than ready to get my blue mind on in April, after three weeks of safer-at-home. One night, I dreamed about busting my pontoon off the Boat Center storage lot and pulling her down the highway still in blue plastic. The next morning, Bruce said, "Maybe you should just call first." To my surprise, Jake at Skeeter's answered. I arranged for the *Jo Sea* to be delivered as soon as ice went off the lake.

After my second phone conversation with Jake, he asked, "Are you related to the Sees from 617 Harding Street?"

I said, "That was our house till my dad died."

"I live there now."

I exclaimed "No way!" so loudly, I'm sure this young man had to pull the phone away from his ear. I am used to Chippewa connections. Still, this one felt special.

"We love it," Jake said. He told me that when he and his girlfriend first toured Dad's house, Jake's mom—a Thorn girl who grew up down the street and was friends with my siblings—encouraged them to buy the See house. What could I say but "Small world"?

～

On most *Jo Sea* trips, I head toward the widest stretch of Lake Hallie. As the sun goes down, the metal edge of a faraway dock turns golden, then on fire. Everything looks different from the height of a pontoon. This may have been part of what inspired

Minnesota farmer Ambrose Weeres, who in 1952 developed a prototype—a wooden platform on top of two steel barrels—based on a seafaring design used for thousands of years. He later opened Weeres Pontoons, the first-ever American pontoon company. His family-friendly vessels were an easy sell: floating on a tippy fishing boat versus a stable pontoon is like the difference between walking on a gangplank or a deck.

One late afternoon, my friend Karen and I lumber along slowly in the *Jo Sea*; even kayakers pass us by. At seventy-nine acres, Lake Hallie is so small, we loop around twice just to feel like we've been somewhere. As we pass Karen's childhood home, her mom comes out to see us. Helen stands in the yard, barefoot and waving.

"Want a ride?" Karen yells.

"No," her mom calls back. Still, Helen walks closer to shore. She recently gave me the greatest compliment: "No one loves Lake Hallie like Patti." That's something coming from an eighty-year-old who's lived on this lake for seventy-four years.

Karen yells to her, "Meet us on Larry's dock."

Helen does. Karen helps her mom aboard.

I steer us over to where Helen grew up: the farm her parents, Clark and Carol Hughes, bought in 1946. Karen's brother owns the house now; Helen still owns the dilapidated barn, the oldest structure on Lake Hallie.

We drift past the Clark Hughes Boat Landing, named for her dad, who donated the land. Helen tells us she can't remember the last time she cruised the lake. It's been decades or more. At sunset, we take in the spectacular view of her old homestead from the middle of Lake Hallie. I can see in Helen's eyes what none of us has to say.

Patti Barge

How will we remember the pandemic summer of 2020: a time when nothing happened or everything did? Out here on Lake Hallie, it was our summer of social distancing on a party barge—an oxymoron, I know. My pontoon came in the same condition as my first pair of jeans and my first car: used. This summer, my Sun Tracker has been the go-to gathering place for family and friends, just a few at a time. My husband calls it the "Patti Barge."

Guests sit on the front benches, and Bruce and I sit at the other end, more than six feet apart. He and I are both in vulnerable groups, a phrase that meant nothing to me five months ago, like that other expression I've come to despise: the new normal. Due to the coronavirus, everything in the Chippewa Valley was on pause through May, but by June we hit "play" again. We often get together with folks who take similar precautions, like masking up for quick trips to grocery and drug stores. My asthmatic sister and her grandson picnic and fish on the pontoon. The high school friend I see once a year gets dropped off for an afternoon booze cruise for two.

I feel safe hosting simply because of the pontoon's size.

In mid-August, my son visits with his buddy on a stopover during their 3,700-mile motorcycle trek, a last hurrah for Alex between deployments. Their goal: ride from where he lives on the southern US border in El Paso to the northern border and back again. So far, he and Greg have ridden through eight states and have been exposed to more people than I've encountered this year. We pontoon, Alex's first time since I bought the boat from him. "What did you do with my waterproof speakers?" he asks me. The boat *is* a little less tricked out now.

As we chug along, he plays Lake Hallie tour guide for Greg. The kid I thought never paid attention to anything I said is now a man retelling my old stories. I am already dreading Alex's next mission and not laying eyes on him for over a year. I will see Alex a few more times before his official departure. Still, today as he leaves, he says to me, "Can I hug you if I hold my breath?" This heartbreaking request is not in my parenting or COVID-19 playbook. I embrace him, turn my face, never want to let go.

⌒

Before Bruce's son Noah visits us, he goes for a COVID-19 swab within an hour of arriving in Eau Claire from the Democratic Republic of the Congo, where he lives. Two days later: negative test results. Bruce holds Noah in a bear hug.

Noah comes home about every six months, but this trip we feel especially fortunate to have him here. Since March, he has been isolating in a compound with his wife, a United Nations migration official in charge of coronavirus relief for the Congo, a country that vigilantly fights Ebola outbreaks.

As we putter along on Lake Hallie, Noah says, "It's weird just to be—" he pauses and looks around, "out." He talks for an hour straight.

Bruce has taught me that we can't constantly worry over adult children. Still, he tells me the litany of dangers he thinks about for Noah: measles, kidnapping, malaria, rebel groups, dengue fever, armed conflict in the streets, and parasitic worms. As the mother of a soldier, I have my own list. No matter how old our children are, naming the threats gives us a sense that maybe we can keep them away.

A few weeks ago, my nephew and his pregnant wife visited for a pontoon ride. A first baby is an exciting but scary time for everyone. In the midst of a pandemic? Really frightening. Twenty-nine summers ago, four days after bringing my son home from the hospital, Jeffrey Dahmer was arrested. While I held newborn Alex close, I watched those unimaginable horrors unfold on the nightly news, a lesson in how bliss and devastation coexist in the world, as they always have.

Tonight, before Mitch and Abby arrive, Bruce warns me that we will not be cruising far from home with a woman who is almost nine months along. He gets his wish. My outboard is wonky, so the four of us sit on the pontoon docked in front of our house—a little like camping in the backyard but still fun. We have drinks and watch the eagles dive into Lake Hallie for their dinner.

I hand Abby the baby card I made with a picture of infant Mitch and a much older picture of his dad (my brother) and his grandfather (my dad). Earlier today, I looked through my jumble of old photographs and considered what these four generations of Sees lived through. The Great Depression, four wars, a polio epidemic, assassinations of leaders, the civil rights movement. There were many other terrors and struggles, but like most Americans, my family posed for the camera then carried on.

And so it was 102 years ago. Some babies born during or just after the influenza pandemic of 1918 later became great influencers: Jackie Robinson and J. D. Salinger, Eva Gabor and Nat King Cole, Pete Seeger and Ann Landers, Katherine Johnson and Billy Graham. A few are still kicking at 101 years old: environmentalist James Lovelock, actor Nehemiah Persoff, and film producer Anne Buydens.

Every day, the world as we knew it seems to fall apart a little bit more. Still, Mitch and Abby's Griffin David See and many other babies like him make their way here anyway.

The Heart Has Many Doors

When I was dating the man who would become my husband, I asked his middle son if he was tired of me hanging out at their house so often. "I like having you around," Dan said. "You're . . ." My relationship with Bruce's children did not hinge on this one exchange, but years later I remember how Dan's words hung in the air above us.

"You're really cheerful," he finally said. What teenager uses that term? I still get teary thinking of the moment I knew I'd won over a Taylor kid; the other two soon followed. Being a stepparent is a bit like playing the role of a favorite sister-in-law: you may not have shared the same womb or childhood history, but you still adore each other. Being a stepmom to three "bonus" kids reminds me of the Emily Dickinson line: "The heart has many doors."

~

A friend once called me the life of the party. I teased, "It's the beer, Mary." Truth is, I pride myself on being not just a happy person but also someone who tries to spread that joy.

I was not always this way. As a sad-sack kid, my feelings were easily hurt, usually by one of my seven older siblings or a mean girl at school. When I cried to my mom, she pulled me onto the wide expanse of her lap and said, "You need to toughen up."

Little by little, I did. When I'm upset, I still hear her voice in my head.

If we compare ourselves to characters in *Winnie the Pooh*, I am definitely like Tigger, bounding with endless optimism and pluck. Not that annoying you-betcha energy but full-on life-source glee. Even my blood type is B positive.

Still, 2020 challenged me to the bone. I see how it has worn down the Piglets (constant worriers) and the Eeyores (diehard pessimists). More than one-third of Americans acknowledge that COVID-19 has affected their mental health. Isolation and anxiety are a terrible combination.

Experts say the majority of adults experience "posttraumatic growth," an increase in well-being after a crisis. Consider how a job loss can lead to an unexpected, more satisfying career path or how an illness can bring a family closer together. Resilient people recognize they always have a choice in how they react to difficult situations. That sense of control is what Holocaust survivor and psychiatrist Viktor Frankl called "tragic optimism."

The pandemic is not over, but we can anticipate an end. This is what I'm primed for in 2021. Cultivating positive energy takes a blend of realism and hope, compassion and thanks. Still, Yale University professor Laurie Santos says bluntly, "Our minds suck at happiness. They're naturally wired for survival. . . . You have to work at happiness."

Recently, a team of "genetics of joy" experts discovered 304 "happy genes" built into our DNA. That's no surprise to those of us who live among Tiggers.

Dr. Sonja Lyubomirsky conducts research on what she calls "the architecture of sustainable happiness." Half of the joy we feel is based on genetics, so that means all of us have a predetermined set point that governs how content we are. People tend to return to that level no matter what happens to them. Lyubomirsky says,

"Truly happy individuals construe life events and daily situations in ways that seem to maintain their happiness." In other words, half-full folks always report that their glasses are midway to the top. Half-empties? Well, we all know what they see.

Surprisingly, just 10 percent of our joyfulness can be attributed to external circumstances. That leaves a whopping 40 percent of our own gladness or misery within our control. There are many ways to increase our contentment. Some swear by exercising or spending time in nature, talking to friends or helping others. Science supports that the simple act of gratitude—focusing on what we do have rather than what we do not—reaps rewards people often cannot imagine.

The night before this past Thanksgiving, I received a text from a friend I see once a summer. Lori wrote, "Thanks for being in my life. Hope you find joy this holiday season."

Though sad about spending the day without a packed house, I remembered what a typical Thanksgiving would be like: many hectic meals with different sides of the family. We'd be together, but likely no one would say anything affectionate in a crowd, least of all me.

Lori's message prompted me to send a short text the next morning to my loved ones: "I am thankful for a sister (or brother or niece or nephew or in-law or son or daughter or friend) like you." I copied and pasted over forty times.

My very first response made me question reaching out. "Day drink much?" my nephew shot back.

Nope, Mitch, not at eight thirty in the morning, even on a holiday. Other texts soon followed: "What a thoughtful greeting" and "I am the grateful one."

I received the stoic Midwestern "Back atcha" twice from people who don't know each other—also a "same here" and an "Aww, thank you" and a "You make our family so fun."

One friend wrote: "One day we will have a joyful reunion."

One in-law texted, "You are my favorite. . . . Shhh, don't tell the others." This long-standing family joke likely *would* have been uttered across the table if we were celebrating in person, but only to get a laugh.

After doing research on happiness, I took my remote gratitude a step further. I recently sent New Year's postcards to loved ones with short paragraphs describing what I appreciate about them. For instance, one to my outspoken sister who makes me want to be bolder; one to my stepdaughter, Laura, and her husband who transformed their dream wedding into a safe celebration; others to friends who illuminate any room.

I realize I won't receive the immediate responses I did to my Thanksgiving messages. Though entertaining and sometimes affirming, that's not really the point.

Over a month ago, when I texted Dan that I was thankful for a stepson like him, he wrote back to me: "You are one of the best things to happen to our family."

I teased back, "What do you mean 'one of'?"

"Well," he wrote, "you know Laura and Ben picked a really awesome dog."

Witness to History

Chippewa County reported its first coronavirus death on October 10, 2020, a dreaded but expected event after Eau Claire County's first in June. By November, local intensive care unit beds were full, but what frightened me even more occurred in December: a nationwide casket shortage.

My minor hassles—staying home more than I would have liked, wearing a face covering in public—are nothing compared to the tremendous losses so many have faced. Over and over, we see how those who carry the heaviest burdens often have the smallest safety nets.

My older sister and I have been in each other's "bubble" since I was born. Now, each weekend we catch up in her living room, my only inside social interaction throughout the winter. I share my local newspapers with her, so I deliver what I call "a bag of old news." She tests positive for COVID-19 on a Saturday night before Christmas. The first few scary days after her diagnosis, I pray she will be one of the lucky mild cases and not one of the gasping, the intubated, the long haulers, the dead. I call her every day. "No cough," she reports. "Feels like a bad cold." She loses her sense of smell and taste, a telltale symptom that will last long past summer. She took the same precautions as I did; we all play coronavirus roulette.

Sometime after the new year begins, Bruce tells me he thinks he'll die before the pandemic ends. I playfully slap him. Still, he seems just fine with his daily routine: write in the morning, check email, work out for a few hours, shower, put on clean sweatpants, have a drink and then dinner, read in the chair, watch a movie, fall asleep. Repeat. He goes weeks without talking to anyone but me. We live in ruts, safe and happy.

One Monday, he doesn't hear me ask him to put some grocery items on his list. When he comes home without what I want, we trade back-and-forth barbs. Me with words, Bruce with looks. He finally says, "You're dangerously close to buying your own beer." I huff down the hall to my office and close the door. There at my desk, laughter starts as a tickle in my throat and then erupts. I apologize to him and say in his deep, calm voice, "You're dangerously close to buying your own beer." We howl at that for days.

Bruce buys piña colada ice cream bars, even though they were not on the list. Each night when he eats one, I sing lines from "Escape (The Piña Colada Song)." Tuesday: "I was tired of my lady; we'd been together too long." Wednesday: "If you like . . . gettin' caught in the rain." Thursday: "If you're not into yoga." Friday: "If you have half a brain."

Now he buys strawberry flavored.

One weekend, I take Bruce's books off the shelves to dust and rearrange. All 813 of them. The faded stamp "Sunny Times Sanatorium" inside one tome makes me wonder about the former owner; the inscriptions from Bruce's old girlfriends ("love always and forever") make me smile. I open a Jack Gilbert collection to a page that reads: "We think of lifetimes as mostly the exceptional and sorrows. . . . The uncommon parts. But the best is often when nothing is happening." Welcome to our world.

Tonight, Bruce kicks my butt at War. Neither of us have played this card game since we had small children. It's February. We're trying new ways to entertain each other. I tell him, "That's the funniest thing you've ever said." The next day we can't recall what it was.

We get through the winter of 2020–2021 the way we've gotten through every other winter: hunkered down with reading materials and multiple remotes. Each Sunday night, I tape a handwritten schedule to the front of the fridge so I can build my life around these two weekly basketball staples, the Badgers and the Celtics.

While my Facebook friends take up piano or purge every closet or bake so much sourdough they beg for people to take bread off their hands, I transition from 2020 articles like "6 Ways to Turn Self-Isolation into Self-Improvement" to 2021's "Stop Trying to Be Productive." The world may have shut down, but for many of us here on Lake Hallie, life goes on as usual. A few weeks after our long stretch of frigid February temperatures, the lake melts in only four days, faster and earlier than we've ever seen. The great blue heron arrives from Florida in early March—just what we need when we need it. Bruce and I stand at the window and watch its graceful shrugs in the shallows, its slow-motion steps toward slippery prey.

I visit my across-the-lake neighbor Helen. We chat at her kitchen table, and she nibbles on the oatmeal cookies I made. Soon she's dialing the phone. "Larry would love to see you," she tells me before saying into the receiver: "Come over right now. We have company." Pause. "It's just Patti."

Two minutes later, Larry walks across his yard to Helen's. I haven't seen either of them indoors for over a year. He sits next to me. "I got the shot," he says. "Me too," I tell him.

"No different than when we all got the polio vaccine," Larry says to Helen. What these two octogenarians have lived through.

In April, I go to the Leinie Lodge. Vaccinated? Then come celebrate with a complimentary pint. "Beer and Shots" is a genius marketing campaign. Bruce and I are two of the first 1,867 people who sign up online. The maximum number for the giveaway reflects the year Leinenkugel's began brewing. Also genius.

One hundred years from now, if Leinenkugel's Brewing Company commemorates the end of this pandemic, how quaint it will seem to future Chippewa Valley residents—perhaps zooming around on their hovercrafts—that back in 2021 people toasted their vaccinations with a glass of Leinie's. Today I know: I am a witness to history. We show our vaccination certificates, take off our masks, and drink the best kind of beer. Chippewa-made, ice-cold, and free.

Acknowledgments

Most of these pieces originated as columns in the Eau Claire *Leader-Telegram*'s Sawdust Stories series. Thank you to past editor Gary Johnson and current editor Matt Milner. I am indebted to reporter Julian Emerson for recruiting me as a columnist. Other pieces first appeared on *Wisconsin Life*—thanks to Erika Janik and Maureen McCollum—and in *Volume One Magazine*—thanks to Nick Meyer, Tom Giffey, and Rebecca Mennecke.

I am grateful to Kate Thompson at the Wisconsin Historical Society Press, who selected my manuscript; to Liz Wyckoff, who worked her magic on line-by-line edits; and to the production and marketing teams, who created a beautiful book.

This collection would not be possible without my husband, Bruce Taylor, who is my first and best audience. His poet's eye for exactly the right word and his keen ear for rhythm make me a better writer. My parents, Joe and Virgie See, both of them lifelong storytellers, would have loved to see some of their own tales in print. More than anything, they might appreciate a book that had in its title "fix-it guys" (my dad, the best handyman around) and "barflies" (my mom, the tavern Shake-a-Day queen). I was always proud to be the youngest of eight children. After our parents died, I found renewed gratitude for my siblings—Sharon, Jackie, Mary, Juliann, Joey, Geralynn, and David—who anchor me in place and buoy me up, often without knowing it.

My neighbors—especially Larry, Dave and Marion, and Helen and Jerry—have offered me their kindness and their love for Lake Hallie. Throughout these pages, I share my best friend and favorite barfly, Karen. Fortunately, I still get her all to myself at my kitchen counter, once a week or so for beer.

Notes

If She Dies, She Dies

3   Simone Torn, "'Winona Forever': Johnny Depp Explains Why He Got His 'Winona Ryder' Tattoo," *Showbiz CheatSheet*, March 6, 2021, www.cheatsheet.com/entertainment/winona-forever -johnny-depp-explains-why-he-got-his-winona-ryder-tattoo.html/.

4   Chris Knutsen and David Kuhn, *Committed: Men Tell Stories of Love, Commitment, and Marriage* (New York: Bloomsbury, 2005).

Cautionary Tales

14   Pam Zaemisch, "80-Year-Old Survives Fall through Ice," *Chippewa Herald-Telegram*, December 20, 1993.

Groundhog Wars

17–18   "Groundhog Day and History," City of Sun Prairie, Wisconsin, accessed February 2, 2021, www.cityofsunprairie.com/840/ Groundhog-Day.

18   Wesley Kempton, "Pennsylvania—Not the Groundhog Capital of the World?" KOWB, February 1, 2012, https://kowb1290.com/ pennsylvania-not-the-groundhog-capital-of-the-world/.

19   "Nuisance, Urban and Damaging Wildlife," Wisconsin Department of Natural Resources, accessed February 2, 2021, https:// dnr.wisconsin.gov/topic/WildlifeHabitat/damage.

Never Afraid

24   Mark Gunderman, "Clark Hughes, Prominent Hallie Landowner, Dies at 91," *Chippewa Herald*, June 7, 2000, https://chippewa .com/clark-hughes-prominent-hallie-landowner-dies-at/article _42aaeac0-8ad9-5d80-8ddc-af9ae0607557.html.

Living on Summer Time

27   Natasha Ishak, "This Small Norwegian Island, Where the Sun Doesn't Set for 69 Days, Wants to Abolish Time," *All That's Interesting*, June 20, 2019, https://allthatsinteresting.com/ sommaroy-island-abolish-time.

27 Anna Schaverien, "Will a Norwegian Island be the First in the World to Go 'Time-free'?" *The Independent*, July 4, 2019, www .independent.co.uk/news/world/norway-sommaroy-island-time -free-zone-summer-daytime-sun-a8985886.html.

Egg Laying

32–33 Jennifer Callaghan, "Native Animal of the Month: Common Snapping Turtle," Urban Ecology Center, January 12, 2015, https://urbanecologycenter.org/blog/native-animal-of-the -month-common-snapping-turtle.html.

Forward

37 Troy Brownfield, "The 50 State Mottos, Ranked," *Saturday Evening Post*, March 25, 2015, www.saturdayeveningpost.com/ 2019/03/the-50-state-mottos-ranked/.

37–38 Wisconsin Historical Society, "Odd Wisconsin: Origin of Wisconsin's 'Forward' Motto," *Wisconsin State Journal*, October 12, 2010, https://madison.com/wsj/news/local/odd-wisconsin -origin-of-wisconsins-forward-motto/article_5aa2bde4-d586 -11df-bd79-001cc4c002e0.html.

39 "Car Fatally Injures Sherry Farmer: I. Weinfurter, 47, Hit While Crossing Road," Wisconsin Rapids *Daily Tribune*, April 10, 1940, p. 1, www.newspapers.com/clip/10639688/weinfurter-ignatz -the-daily-tribune/.

A Brief Story

49 "England Based Flying Fortress Pilot Missing" and "Missing Aviator Returns to Duty," ChippewaValleyWWII, accessed December 12, 2011, www.chippewavalleyww2.org/Veterans/S/Sa/ SabinMyronE/SabinMyronE.htm (site discontinued).

49 Obituary of Myron Edward "Pete/Bud" Sabin, *Chippewa Herald*, August 8, 2011, https://chippewa.com/news/local/obituaries/ myron-edward-pete-bud-sabin/article_8c63d972-c1de-11e0 -b72e-001cc4c002e0.html.

Fine Music

50 Katie Vagnino, "Where FM Means Fine Music," *Volume One Magazine*, August 24, 2016, https://volumeone.org/sites/chippewafalls/ articles/2016/08/26/206291-where-fm-means-fine-music.

51   Anne Sexton, "Music Swims Back to Me," *The Complete Poems of Anne Sexton* (Boston: Houghton Mifflin, 1981).

Mourning Portrait

56   Bethan Bell, "Taken from Life: The Unsettling Art of Death Photography," BBC News, June 5, 2016, www.bbc.com/news/uk-england-36389581.

Secret Spaces

59–60   The Kitchen Sisters, "Poet Emily Dickinson Was a Much Loved Baker," *Morning Edition*, National Public Radio, December 27, 2016, www.npr.org/2016/12/27/507063472/poet-emily-dickinson-was-a-much-loved-baker.

Tavern Tour

66   "Brewing and Prohibition," Wisconsin Historical Society, accessed July 14, 2020, www.wisconsinhistory.org/Records/Article/CS425.

66   Jim Draeger and Mark Speltz, *Bottoms Up: A Toast to Wisconsin's Historic Bars and Breweries* (Madison: Wisconsin Historical Society Press, 2012).

67   Bill Moen and Doug Davis, *Badger Bars & Tavern Tales: An Illustrated History of Wisconsin Saloons* (St. Germain, Wis.: Guest Cottage Press, 2003).

Why I Revere My Septic Guy

70   C. Claiborne Ray, "The Flush Is Just the Beginning: What Happens After They Clean Out Your Septic Tank? Well, It's Complicated," *New York Times*, July 23, 2018, www.nytimes.com/2018/07/23/science/septic-waste-disposal.html.

71   "A Brief History of the Septic Tank," B&B Pumping, December 31, 2019, www.bbpumpingtx.com/blog/a-brief-history-of-the-septic-tank/.

72   "Private Onsite Wastewater Treatment Systems," Chippewa County, accessed February 19, 2020, www.co.chippewa.wi.us/government/planning-zoning/program-information/powts.

72   Frank Aguirre, "Dignity of the Septic Guy: Part One," *Pumper*, February 17, 2014, www.pumper.com/online_exclusives/2014/02/dignity_of_the_septic_guy_part_one.

The Eagle Man of Eau Claire

75   Walt Whitman, "The Dalliance of Eagles," *The Complete Poems* (New York: Penguin Classics, 2005).

75–76   "Summary of the Endangered Species Act," United States Environmental Protection Agency, accessed June 5, 2019, www.epa.gov/laws-regulations/summary-endangered-species-act.

76   "Eagles in Wisconsin," Wisconsin Department of Natural Resources, accessed June 5, 2019, https://dnr.wisconsin.gov/topic/WildlifeHabitat/baldeagle.html.

77   "Northern States Bald Eagle Recovery Plan," United States Fish and Wildlife Service, July 29, 1983, ecos.fws.gov/docs/recovery_plan/060309b.pdf.

77   Jonathan Wood, "The New Endangered Species Act Rules, Explained," Property and Environment Resource Center, August 14, 2019, www.perc.org/2019/08/14/the-new-endangered-species-act-rules-explained.

Date Cutters

78–79   Dan Lyksett, "Memorial Stone Carver Learned to Read Life Stories Between the Markers' Lines," Eau Claire *Leader-Telegram*, September 17, 2016, www.leadertelegram.com/News/Front-Page/2016/09/17/Engraved-with-love.html.

79   *Into the Night: Portraits of Life and Death*, directed by Helen Whitney, aired March 26, 2018, on PBS, www.intothenightdoc.com/.

80   Max Martinson, "The Last Call: Local Music Great Krause Releases Final Album," *Volume One Magazine*, July 13, 2017, http://volumeone.org/articles/2017/07/13/19823_the_last_call.

The Bird Man of Chippewa Falls

82–83   Shannon Tompkins, "Bird Bands Tell Stories to Science, Hunters," *Houston Chronicle*, December 3, 2016, www.chron.com/sports/outdoors/article/Bird-bands-tell-stories-to-science-hunters-10689755.php.

83 Bob Green, "A Country Doctor Can't Forget His 40 Years of House Calls," *Wall Street Journal.* February 8, 2018, www.wsj .com/articles/a-country-doctor-cant-forget-his-40-years-of -house-calls-1518134157.

84 Charles Hillinger, "No Beep-Beep, Barely Even a Cheep from Rogue Road Runner," *Los Angeles Times,* November 28, 1990, www.latimes.com/archives/la-xpm-1990-11-28-mn-4911-story .html.

85 Mary-Russell Roberson, "Charles Kemper '40: Birds and Survival," *Duke Magazine,* April 1, 2007, https://alumni.duke.edu/ magazine/articles/charles-kemper-40.

85 Joe Knight, "Longtime Bird Counter Cutting Back," Eau Claire *Leader-Telegram,* January 1, 2013, www.leadertelegram.com/ news/front-page/longtime-bird-counter-cutting-back/article _b892a049-ead9-5822-b3df-d24c8cd6315a.html.

85 Christy Ullrich Barcus, "Audubon's Christmas Bird Count Turns 115: Why Does It Matter?" *National Geographic,* December 25, 2014, www.nationalgeographic.com/animals/article/141227 -christmas-bird-count-anniversary-audubon-animals-science.

85 Rod Stetzer, "Plans for Kemper's Woods Taking Flight," *Chippewa Herald,* April 21, 2007, https://chippewa.com/news/plans-for -kempers-woods-taking-flight/article_16544316-7ee3-5c31-9275 -a753476d19a8.html.

Our Miss Victory
86–87 Harold 'Diz' Kronenberg, "World War II's Impact on Eau Claire," Chippewa Valley World War II, November 2002, chippewavalley ww2.org (site discontinued).

88 Redd Evans and John Jacob Loeb, "Rosie the Riveter," Paramount Music Corporation of New York, 1942.

88–90 Penny Colman, *Rosie the Riveter: Women Working on the Home Front in World War II* (New York: Yearling Publishing, 1998).

90 Erick Trickey, "Rosie the Riveter Isn't Who You Think She Is," *The Washington Post,* September 3, 2018, www.washingtonpost.com/ news/retropolis/wp/2018/09/03 rosie-the-riveter-isnt-who-you -think-she-is/.

Lake Hallie Spirits

91   Leonora Desar, "Secret Life of a Ghost Hunter," *Narratively*, October 28, 2013, https://narratively.com/the-secret-life-of-a-ghost-hunter/.

92   "Time Capsule: Hallie Golf Course has Long History," *Chippewa Herald*, August 25, 2018, https://chippewa.com/lifestyles/local/time-capsule-hallie-golf-course-has-long-history/article_fd9b96ee-34e8-5848-818a-20b13a7a0b79.html.

Fish Fry at Irvine

99   "Irvine Ghost Pub," Wisconsin Haunted Houses, accessed October 31, 2019, www.wisconsinhauntedhouses.com/real-haunt/irvine-ghost-pub.html.

99   Candice Novitzke, "Checking in on Favorite Haunts in Chippewa Falls," *Chippewa Herald*, October 30, 2008, https://chippewa.com/news/checking-in-on-favorite-haunts-in-chippewa-falls/article_75470f0d-cf57-5800-b5a9-b25015fdfdcc.html.

99   "William Irvine," Historical Markers Database, accessed October 31, 2019, www.hmdb.org/m.asp?m=38788.

His Shirt Was Always Tucked In

108   Dave Roos, "How Obituaries Went from Dry Death Notices to Tributes to Truth," *How Stuff Works*, December 3, 2019, https://people.howstuffworks.com/culture-traditions/funerals/obituary-history.htm.

108–9   Stephen Levine, "Let It Shine," *The Sun*, May 2016, www.thesunmagazine.org/issues/485/let-it-shine.

No Green Bananas

119   Annie Dillard, *The Writing Life* (New York: Harper Perennial, 2013).

Everything Must Go

122   Shane Cashman, "When You Die, I'll Be There to Take Your Stuff," *Narratively*, September 12, 2016, https://narratively.com/when-you-die-ill-be-there-to-take-your-stuff/.

122   Patrick Sisson, "Self-storage: How Warehouses for Personal Junk Became a $38 Billion Industry," *Curbed*, March 27, 2018, www

.curbed.com/2018/3/27/17168088/cheap-storage-warehouse
-self-storage-real-estate.

Cribbage Family

126   "History of Cribbage," Stanwardine, accessed January 18, 2019,
       www.stanwardine.com/HistoryOfGame.htm.

126   Brett and Kate McKay, "The Manly History of Cribbage and How
       to Play the Game," *The Art of Manliness*, November 28, 2012,
       www.artofmanliness.com/articles/the-manly-history-of-cribbage
       -and-how-to-play-the-game/.

Goodbye 617

131   Anne Lamott, "12 Truths I Learned from Life and Writing,"
       TED conference, April 2017, video, 15:45, www.ted.com/talks/
       anne_lamott_12_truths_i_learned_from_life_and_writing
       ?language=en.

Firebugs

134   Natalie Wolchover, "Why We Are Drawn to Fire," *Live Science*,
       April 23, 2012, www.livescience.com/19853-fire-fascination.html.

134   Carolyn Gregoire, "The Evolutionary Reason Why We Love Sit-
       ting by A Crackling Fire," *The Huffington Post*, November 18, 2014,
       www.huffpost.com/entry/the-evolutionary-reason-w_n_6171508.

136   "The Science Behind Fireflies," PestWorld.org, accessed on July
       17, 2019, www.pestworld.org/news-hub/pest-articles/the-science
       -behind-fireflies/.

136   "Disappearing Fireflies," Firefly Conservation and Research, accessed
       on July 17, 2019, www.firefly.org/why-are-fireflies-disappearing.html.

For All the Handy Men I've Loved

140   Tracy Moore, "Men Don't Know How to Fix or Build Anything
       Anymore: An Investigation," *Mel Magazine*, accessed November
       15, 2020, https://melmagazine.com/en-us/story/men-dont
       -know-how-to-fix-or-build-anything-anymore-an-investigation.

140   Andy Hinds, "What Being a Handyman Has Taught Me About
       Male Insecurity," *The Atlantic*, March 28, 2013, www.theatlantic
       .com/sexes/archive/2013/03/what-being-a-handyman-has
       -taught-me-about-male-insecurity/274426/.

The Cruelest Month

143   Scott Anderson, "Why Has the 2018-19 Wisconsin Winter Been So Bad?" *Patch News*, March 7, 2019, https://patch.com/wisconsin/mountpleasantwhy-has-2018-19-wisconsin-winter-been-so-bad.

143–44   "4 Reasons Climate Change is Here, Even Though It's Cold," Environmental Defense Fund, accessed on January 29, 2019, www .edf.org/card/4-reasons-climate-change-still-happening-despite -cold-weather?card=4.

143–44   Ethan Siegel, "This is Why Global Warming Is Responsible for Freezing Temperatures Across the U.S.," *Forbes*, January 30, 2019, www.forbes.com/sites/startswithabang/2019/01/30/this-is-why -global-warming-is-responsible-for-freezing-temperatures-across -the-usa/#6808d566d8cf.

144   Doug Criss and Judson Jones, "Here's Your Answer When Someone Asks 'How Can It Be So Cold If There's Global Warming?'" CNN, November 12, 2019, www.cnn.com/2019/01/29/ weather/global-warming-cold-weather-explainer-wxc-trnd/ index.html.

Our Old Town

148–49   John Tierney, "What Is Nostalgia Good For? Quite a Bit, Research Shows," *New York Times*, July 8, 2013, www.nytimes.com/ 2013/07/09/science/what-is-nostalgia-good-for-quite-a-bit -research-shows.html?_r=0.

148–49   John Hildebrand, *Long Way Round: Through the Heartland by River* (Madison: University of Wisconsin Press, 2019).

Shake-a-Day

151–54   Ray Oldenburg, *The Great Good Place: Cafés, Coffee Shops, Bookstores, Bars, Hair Salons, and Other Hangouts at the Heart of a Community* (Cambridge, MA: Da Capo Press, 1999).

152   Robert Simonson, "How Bar Dice Became a Wisconsin Institution," *Punch*, June 18, 2018, https://punchdrink.com/articles/ how-to-play-bar-dice-wisconsin-drinking-game/.

153   Jim Draeger and Mark Speltz, *Bottoms Up: A Toast to Wisconsin's Historic Bars and Breweries* (Madison: Wisconsin Historical Society Press, 2012).

Get Your Blue Mind On

156–57   Wallace Nichols, *Blue Mind: The Surprising Science That Shows How Being Near, In, On, or Under Water Can Make You Happier, Healthier, More Connected, and Better at What You Do* (New York: Back Bay Books, 2015).

157–58   "History of the Pontoon," *Pontoon and Deck Boat Magazine*, August 2013, www.pdbmagazine.com/2013/08/history-of-the -pontoon.

The Heart Has Many Doors

163   Lisa Capretto, "The Reason Some People Just Seem Happier Than Others," *The Huffington Post*, December 7, 2015, www .huffpost.com/entry/the-reason-some-people-are-happier _n_5661d1d5e4b072e9d1c5ed80.

163   Sari Harrar, "Lessons in Finding Happiness During Hard Times," *AARP Magazine*, June 16, 2020, www.aarp.org/health/healthy -living/info-2020/finding-happiness-during-tough-times.html.

163   Victor Frankl, *Man's Search for Meaning* (Boston: Beacon Press, 2005).

163–64   Adam Sternbergh, "Read This Story and Get Happier: The Most Popular Course at Yale Teaches How to be Happy. We Took It for You," *The Cut*, May 2018, www.thecut.com/2018/05/how-to-be -happy.html.

163–64   Lisa Truesdale, "Why Some People Are Happier than Others (and What to Do If You're Not)," *delicious living*, October 9, 2017, www.deliciousliving.com/health/why-some-people-are-happier -others-and-what-do-if-you-re-not/.

Witness to History

167   Jack Gilbert, "Highlights and Interstices," *The Great Fires* (New York: Alfred A. Knopf, 1994).

168   "The Pandemic: One Man's Appreciation," GarrisonKeillor.com, accessed on January 20, 2021, www.garrisonkeillor.com/the -pandemic-one-mans-appreciation/.

About the Author

Patti See writes a monthly Sawdust Stories column for the Eau Claire *Leader-Telegram* and *Country Today*. Her work has appeared in *Salon Magazine, Women's Studies Quarterly, Journal of Developmental Education, Wisconsin People & Ideas, The Southwest Review, HipMama,* and *Inside HigherEd,* as well as many other magazines and anthologies. She has been a regular contributor to *Wisconsin Life* on Wisconsin Public Radio. Her blog, *Our Long Goodbye: One Family's Experiences with Alzheimer's,* has been read in over one hundred countries. She is also the co-author, with Bruce Taylor, of a textbook, *Higher Learning: Reading and Writing about College* and the author of a poetry collection, *Love's Bluff.*